GET LOW

GET LOW

REFLECTIONS ON PRIDE AND HUMILITY

JACK WISDOM

Whitecaps Media
Houston

Whitecaps Media
Houston, Texas
whitecapsmedia.com

Get Low: Reflections on Pride and Humility
© 2013 Jack Wisdom
All rights reserved

ISBN-13: 978-0-9836825-8-5

FIRST EDITION

Cover designed by Stephanie W. Dicken. Book designed and edited by Kit Sublett for Whitecaps Media. Main body composed in Minion Pro, 11/14. Titles are in Blanch, a font designed by Atipus of Barcelona

Unless otherwise noted, all Scripture quotations are the author's own translations

Scripture quotations marked "The Voice" taken from The Voice™. Copyright © 2008 by Ecclesia Bible Society. Used by permission. All rights reserved

Printed in the United States of America

*for Diana, Alison, Claire and Josh, who
remind me that I am richly blessed*

*for Gordon Fee, the "scholar on fire,"
who taught me how to read the Bible
for all its worth*

and for Joel, whom I miss

CONTENTS

Introduction 1
Pride 7
Theology 13
History 20
Integrity 26
Industry 34
Prosperity 41
Religiosity 51
Certainty 57
Unity 67
Reality 75
Liberty 83
Family 88
Ideology 95
Celebrity 104
Bravery 110
Mortality 119
Charity 129
Idolatry 135
Authority 142
Anxiety 155
Memory 161
Enmity 170
Adversity 178
Victory 184
Bibliography 201

God's arm has accomplished mighty deeds.
The proud in mind and heart,
God has sent away in disarray.

The rulers from their high positions of power,
God has brought down low.

And those who were humble and lowly,
God has elevated with dignity.
(Luke 1:51–52, "The Voice")

We need to get low.

INTRODUCTION

My family owns a few acres near Hearne, the self-proclaimed "crossroads of Texas." Hearne has three Tex-Mex restaurants (not counting the *panaderia* and the taco truck), two grocery stores, two dollar-style discount stores, two barbecue joints, two auto parts stores, and one bridge that spans railroad tracks and Highway 6. A few years ago, some visionary entrepreneur opened a sports bar in the middle of town. It is not exactly the ESPN Zone, but it seems to be a relatively successful venture. The sports bar serves as a refuge for the men of Hearne. Every Saturday and Sunday during football season, the parking lot of the sports bar is packed with dozens of pick-up trucks and one very old riding lawn mower. Many nights, I have seen the same gentleman wearing a sharp gold blazer and driving his riding lawn mower over the bridge towards the sports bar. I don't know why he drives a lawn mower to the sports bar. He probably does it because he likes sports and/or bars, does not like walking, and does not mind looking ridiculous if that is what it takes to accomplish his mission.

Every time I see that fellow on the lawn mower heading into the heart of Hearne, I think about the so-called triumphal entry of Jesus into Jerusalem:

> Jesus, the disciples, and the great crowds were heading toward Jerusalem when they came to Bethphage on the Mount of Olives. Jesus stopped and beckoned to two of the disciples.
> **Jesus:** Go to the village over there. There you'll find a donkey tied to a post and a foal beside it. Untie them and bring them to Me. If anyone tries to stop you, then tell him. "The Master needs these," and he will send the donkey and foal immediately.
> He sent the disciples on ahead so His entry into Jerusalem could fulfill what the prophet Zechariah had long since foretold: "Tell this to Zion's daughter, 'Look—your King is approaching, seated humbly on a donkey, a young foal, a beast of burden.'"
> So the disciples went off and followed Jesus' instructions. They brought the donkey and foal to Jesus, they spread their cloaks on the animals, and Jesus sat down on them. The great crowd followed suit, laying their cloaks on the road. Others cut leafy branches from the trees and scattered those before Jesus. And the crowds went before Jesus, walked alongside Him, and processed behind—all singing.
> **Crowd:** Hosanna, praises to the Son of David! Blessed is He who comes in the name of the Eternal One! Hosanna in the highest!
> And that is how Jesus came into Jerusalem. The people noticed this strange parade. They wondered who this could be, this humble bearded man on a donkey who incited such songs.
> **Crowd:** This is Jesus, the prophet, from Nazareth in Galilee.[1]

---

[1] Matthew 21:1–11 *(The Voice)*.

Introduction

The whole strange scene was predicted by Zechariah. The shocking point of Zechariah's prophesy is that the King is humble.[2] When the prophet says he comes riding on "an ass," he is contrasting him with "the chariot," "the war horse," and "the battle bow" (Zechariah 9:10). It is the fact that the King is a man of peace that is distinctive. In antiquity, a king would not enter his capital riding on a donkey. He would ride proudly, on a warhorse, or perhaps he would march at the head of his troops.[3]

Jesus came into Jerusalem as a humble King on a donkey, which was "a contradiction in terms."[4] This was the entrance of "a King whose rule does not depend on political and military might," whose "inmost being is humility and meekness," and who is "the exact opposite of the great kings of the world"; a King who "rides on an ass—the mount of the poor, the counter-image of the chariot that he rejects."[5] Moreover, he was not even riding on a well-bred donkey; this donkey is specifically identified as a "beast of burden."[6] It was a lowly animal even by donkey standards.

Because we are so familiar with the story, and relatively unfamiliar with the way great and powerful kings and generals led triumphal processions in antiquity,[7] we may miss the shock value

---

[2] Morris, *The Gospel According to Matthew*, 520.

[3] Ibid., 521.

[4] Ibid.

[5] Ratzinger, *Jesus of Nazareth: From the Baptism in the Jordan to the Transfiguration*, 81.

[6] Morris, *The Gospel According to Matthew*, 521.

[7] Tom Holland offers the following vivid description of a Roman triumphal procession: "Driven through the grateful streets, born on the clamor of deafening applause and acclamation, a general on the day of his triumph

of the ways and means of Jesus' entry into Jerusalem. To correct that problem, try to picture a great modern leader, on his way to a climactic battle or a diplomatic summit, driving a riding lawn mower. Don't picture the great leader operating a sexy new Toro SS 5060 V-Twin Hydrostatic Zero-Turn Riding Mower with Smart Speed™; picture the great leader puttering along on a rusty old junker. That is the way Jesus, the King of kings, entered Jerusalem. In retrospect, it is clear that he could not have accomplished the mission any other way.

The humility of Jesus is not a superfluous detail in the gospel narrative. The humility of Jesus is essential to the gospel. If Jesus lacked humility, there would be no incarnation, no crucifixion, and no redemption. John Howard Yoder's meditation on the downward mobility of God in Jesus—to the point of death on a Roman cross—makes this point well:

> The path of the cross is not an accident. It is not a detour on the way to victory. It is not the bitter that we have to take with the sweet . . . it is not the bad news mixed with the good. It

---

became something more than a citizen, something more even than a man. Not only was he dressed in the gold and purple of a king, but his face was painted red like the holiest statute in Rome, that of Jupiter in the great temple of the Capital. To partake of the divine was a glorious, intoxicating, perilous thing, and during the few brief hours when it was permitted, a general became a spectacle of wonder and edification. To the Roman people who lined the streets to cheer him, he was living reassurance that ambition might indeed be sacred, that in struggling to reach the top, and to achieve great things, a citizen was fulfilling his duty to the Republic and to the gods" (Holland, *Rubicon*, 184–85). See also Yancey, *The Jesus I Never Knew*, 190, describing a Roman triumphal procession, and contrasting Rome's displays of power with Jesus' entry into Jerusalem.

is the good news. Divine self-emptying *is* the gospel. It is the revelation of the way things are.[8]

Augustine of Hippo made the same point over 1,500 years ago:

> What greater mercy is there than this, which caused to descend from heaven the Maker of heaven; which reclothed with an earthly body the One who formed the earth; which made equal to us the One who, from eternity, is the equal of the Father; which imposed "the form of a servant" on the Master of the world—such that the Bread itself was hungry, Fullness itself was thirsty, Power itself was made weak, Health itself was wounded, and Life itself was mortal? And that so that our hunger would be satisfied, so that our dryness would be watered, our weakness supported, our love ignited. What greater mercy than that which presents to us the Creator created; the Master made a slave; the Redeemer sold; the One who exalts, humbled; the One who raises the dead, killed?[9]

Because Jesus humbled himself, there is forgiveness, reconciliation, and a new creation. For those who want to follow Jesus, humility is a non-negotiable necessity. Augustine was emphatic about the necessity of humility:

> Grasp the truth of God by using the way he himself provides, since he sees the weakness in our footsteps. That way consists first, of humility, second, of humility and third, of humility. Unless humility precedes, accompanies and follows up all the

---

[8] Yoder, *He Came Preaching Peace*, 92.
[9] Augustine, *Sermon 207*.

good we accomplish, unless we keep our eyes fixed on it, pride will snatch everything right out of our hands.[10]

This book is about living with humility in a world that has been vandalized by pride. I am convinced that the destructive consequences of pride are evident in every aspect of life, including the way we theologize, the way we consume, the way we give, and the way we work, as well as the way we face adversity, anxiety, death, and doubt. I am equally convinced the way to redeem every aspect of life is the way of humility. In this book, I am trying to make that case.

I am not an expert on the topic. In fact, the folks who know me best will testify that I am uniquely *unqualified* to write about humility. In spite of that—or maybe because of that—I have written this collection of essays for proud people who are called to imitate a humble King. I pray that the Holy Spirit will give us eyes to see the glory of God in the crucified Messiah, and to know that we have been given this treasure in "jars of clay to show that the all-surpassing power is from God and not from us."[11]

---

[10] Augustine, *Letter 118*.

[11] 2 Corinthians 4:7. Unless otherwise noted, all verses are the author's translations.

CHAPTER 1

PRIDE

We live in a rebellious and broken world, and there is a tragic gap between the way things are and the way things ought to be. The New Testament describes this status quo in several ways, including the "world," this "present evil age," and the "dominion of darkness." I translate all of these terms with the phrase "bogus world system."

The bogus world system is bogus because people have turned away from God, and have become enslaved to hostile spiritual powers. The "ruler" of the bogus world system is Satan, the adversary.[1] The bogus world system, therefore, is characterized by the primordial sin that triggered Satan's ill-conceived cosmic rebellion: "the boastful pride of life."[2]

All of us—each in his or her own way—are proud, and the consequences of our collective and personal pride are multifarious

---

[1] John 12:31; 1 Peter 5:8.
[2] 1 John 2:16.

and tragic. Cornelius Platinga defines "sinful human pride" as "that blend of narcissism and conceit that we detest in others and sometimes tenderly protect in ourselves" and asks: "What sin ... causes more wars, envies, fratricides, tyrannies, ethnic cleansings, and general subversions of fellowship? What sin makes God seem more irrelevant?"[3]

C. S. Lewis identifies pride as "the essential vice, the utmost evil." According to Lewis, "unchastity, anger, greed, drunkenness, and all that, are mere fleabites in comparison: it was through pride that the Devil became the Devil. Pride leads to every other vice. It is the complete anti-God state of mind."[4]

Pope Benedict XVI describes pride as "man's real sin, his deepest temptation ... the arrogant presumption of autonomy that leads man to put on airs of divinity, to claim to be his own god."[5]

John Stott's comments about pride are equally strong:

> Pride is more than the first of the seven deadly sins; it is itself the essence of all sin. For it is the stubborn refusal to let God be God, with the corresponding ambition to take his place. It is the attempt to dethrone God and enthrone ourselves. Sin is self-deification.[6]

The Hebrew prophets assailed and lamented pride as the root cause and catastrophic effect of our participation in the cosmic

---

[3] Platinga, *Not the Way It's Supposed to Be*, 81.

[4] Lewis, *Mere Christianity*, 121.

[5] Ratzinger, *Jesus of Nazareth: From the Baptism in the Jordan to the Transfiguration*, 98.

[6] Stott, "Pride, Humility and God," 11.

rebellion.[7] Isaiah contrasts the way things are—we exalt[8] ourselves and advance our interests by any means necessary, including war—and the way things ought to be and will be—"YHWH alone will be exalted" and we will "study war no more."[9] In spite of the clear warnings and compelling visions of the prophets, people and nations persist in the folly and futility of pride. That is the bad news.

The good news is that God has invaded the bogus world system, and—in a demonstration of shocking humility—Jesus disarmed the proud hostile powers by dying on a Roman cross.[10] He invites us to shift our allegiance from the bogus world system to his kingdom, but we must leave our pride behind. To enter God's kingdom, we must imitate the King: we must get low.

The New Testament word for humble, *tapeinos*, literally means low-lying.[11] In Classical Greek, the word was used metaphorically to describe low social position, and the servile, groveling behavior of low-class people.[12] The Greeks, therefore, did not regard it as a virtue to be *tapeinos*.[13] In the New Testament, that perspective changes because the kingdom of God turns the pride-based

---

[7] See, for example, Amos 6:8; Zephaniah 3:11–13; Ezekiel 16:49–50; and Jeremiah 5:29–32.

[8] Multiple Hebrew words are used to convey the idea of pride. Several (*ga'own, ruwm,* and *gabahh*) share the meaning "lift up," "to be high," "to exalt." "Pride," *The Interpreter's Dictionary of the Bible Vol. 3* (Nashville: Abingdon, 1962).

[9] Isaiah 2:6–22.

[10] Colossians 2:15.

[11] "Humility," *Dictionary of New Testament Theology Vol. II* (Grand Rapids: Eerdmans, 1980).

[12] Ibid.

[13] Ibid.

values of the bogus world system upside down. In Mary's song, she celebrates the coming of Jesus, the Son of the Most High, who scatters the proud, topples the mighty, and exalts the lowly.[14]

Nevertheless, nobody was ready for a Messiah who was "meek" and "lowly in heart," but that is exactly what they got.[15] His followers expected him to lead a triumphant military struggle, and some of them actually were eagerly anticipating positions of status and power in the new regime,[16] but Jesus had a radically different plan:

> At that time the disciples came to Jesus and said, "Who is the greatest in the kingdom of heaven?" Then Jesus called a child to him and had him stand among them. "I assure you," he said, "unless you change your ways and become like children, you will never enter the kingdom of heaven." Therefore, whoever humbles himself like this child—this one is the greatest in the kingdom of heaven. Whoever welcomes one child like this in my name welcomes me.[17]

Leon Morris's comments on this passage are worth quoting:

> We should not take this to mean "humbles himself as this little child humbles himself" but rather "humbles himself until he becomes like this little child" . . . In modern Western societies, children are often seen as very important, but in First Century Judaism, they were not . . . In the affairs of men, children were

---

[14] Luke 1:31–32, 51–52.
[15] Matthew 11:29.
[16] Mark 10:37.
[17] Matthew 18:1–5.

unimportant. They could not fight, they could not lead, they had not had time to acquire worldly wisdom, they could not pile up riches, they counted for very little . . . Their smallness made them very humble members of society. Thus, when Jesus says his followers must humble themselves as this little child, he is not uttering a truism, but making a most unexpected pronouncement.[18]

Jesus was not demanding that the disciples make themselves lower than they actually were. He was telling them that they should know—like the child—how lowly they really were. Stott calls humility "nothing but the truth" and "a synonym for honesty."[19] Paradoxically, humility is the only way to greatness in the Kingdom.

After Jesus' death and resurrection, his followers gathered and sang praises to the One who "existed in the form of God," but "humbled himself by becoming obedient to the point of death—even death on a Roman cross."[20] They joyfully sang that Jesus, because he humbled himself, had been "highly exalted" and been given "the Name above all names," YHWH.[21]

They encouraged one another to imitate Jesus in his faithful humility, to be *tapeinophron*, lowly in mind, and they did so with the confidence that God would vindicate them.[22] This is foolish-

---

[18] Morris, *The Gospel According to Matthew*, 185.

[19] Stott, *Christ the Controversialist*, 125.

[20] Philippians 2:8.

[21] Philippians 2:9–11; Fee, *Pauline Christology*, 396. YHWH is the personal name of the God of Israel in the Hebrew Scriptures (see Exodus 3:13–14). Many English translations substitute "the LORD" for the Name.

[22] Philippians 2:1–5.

ness by the standards of the bogus world system, but it is the way of the King and his kingdom. Augustine makes this point well:

> Why are you so proud? God became humble for your sake! Perhaps you would be ashamed to imitate a humble man; then at least imitate a humble God. The Son of God came as a man and became humble ... Pride does its own will: humility does the will of God.[23]

Lord, expose and root out our destructive pride. Correct our thinking so that we esteem all that is truly worthy and so that we remember our place. Teach us how to get low. Amen.

---

[23] Augustine, *Sermon on John 25*.

CHAPTER 2

THEOLOGY

Theology is the study of God. Christian theology is the study of the incomparable God who "spoke through the prophets at different times and in various ways" but revealed himself decisively in His Son,[1] Jesus the Liberating King, the Lamb who was slaughtered.[2]

It is a safe bet that the leading teachers of the Hebrews Scriptures in first century Palestine were not prepared for the Holy One of Israel to reveal himself as a "friend of sinners,"[3] and they certainly were not ready to accept a crucified Messiah. In fact, after Jesus was publicly humiliated and executed, the confident consensus of the theological establishment was that the Crucifixion effectively ended any messianic claims or aspirations relating to Jesus because the Scriptures clearly pronounce that "everyone who is

---

[1] Hebrews 1:1–3.
[2] Revelation 5:12.
[3] Luke 7:34.

hung on a cross is cursed."[4] Given this explicit biblical premise, the logic of the scholars seemed to be irrefutable: 1) The Messiah could not be cursed, 2) Jesus was cursed, therefore 3) Jesus could not be the Messiah. They were suffering from "hardening of the categories."[5]

The point here is not to critique Jewish exegetical methodology. Rather, the point is that God will confound the people who think they have figured him out. Those who teach, study, or debate theology, therefore, should do so with humility. Consider the personal testimony of Augustine:

> My ambition as a youth was to apply to the study of the Holy Scriptures all the refinement of dialectics. I did so, but without the humility of the true searcher. I was supposed to knock at the door so it would open for me. Instead, I was pushing it closed, trying to understand in pride what is only learned in humility.[6]

In First Corinthians, Paul wrote to some folks who were quite impressed with their own theological knowledge relating to spirituality and Christian freedom. Based on their so-called knowledge, they were asserting their right to participate in cultic meals in idols' temples, even though their actions could destroy the faith of a brother or sister.[7] In his response to this particular

---

[4] Deuteronomy 21:23.

[5] I borrowed this phrase from a lecture by Gordon Fee in a New Testament survey class at Gordon-Conwell Seminary in 1980.

[6] Augustine, *Sermon 51*.

[7] Fee, *The First Epistle to the Corinthians*, 361–79. Fee explains the historical context as follows: "In the Corinth of Paul's time, such meals were still the regular practice both at state festivals and private celebrations of various kinds . . . The gods were thought to be present since the meals were held in

Theology

problem, Paul provides a timeless principle: "Knowledge puffs up with pride, but love builds up. If anyone thinks he has arrived at knowledge, he does not yet know as he ought to know, but if anyone loves, this one truly knows."[8]

Gordon Fee comments on the implications of this principle:

> True *gnosis* consists not in the accumulation of so much data, nor even in the correctness of one's theology, but in the fact that one has learned to live in love toward all ... Christian behavior is not predicated on the way of knowledge, which leads to pride and destroys others, but on the way of love, which is in fact the true way of knowledge ... the tyranny of "knowledge" as the basis of Christian ethics has a long and unfortunate history in the church, from which most likely few who read—as well as the one who writes—this commentary are exempt. Once one's theology is properly in hand, it is especially tempting to use it as a club on others. And in this case, it happens from the theological right as well as from the left. This does not mean that knowledge is either irrelevant or unimportant, but it does mean that it cannot serve as the primary basis of Christian behavior. In Christian ethics "knowledge" must always lead to love ... In the Christian faith "knowledge" or "insight" is never an end

---

their honor and sacrifices were made ... Some of the Corinthian believers are among those for whom the gods were a genuine reality while they were pagans ... they may tell their heads all they want that the god is only an idol and that an idol has no genuine reality. The fact is that their former way of life is woven into their consciousness and emotions in such a way that the old associations cannot be thus lightly disregarded. For them to return to the place of their former worship would mean once more to eat as though it were truly being sacrificed to the god."

[8] 1 Corinthians 8:2.

in itself; it is only a means to a greater end, the building up of others.[9]

We should not and cannot abstain from theology. Nor should we conclude that nothing about God is knowable, or that all theological claims and contentions are equally valid or invalid. Among the Corinthians, Paul was "determined to know nothing except [the scandalous narrative of] Jesus the Liberating King and Him crucified,"[10] but Paul expects and assumes that his readers already know many theological facts, including that 1) they (collectively) are God's temple and he is present among them as the Holy Spirit;[11] and 2) each of their physical bodies (individually) is a temple of the Holy Spirit.[12] These amazing facts, however, are not to be known as esoteric mysteries that puff us up with pride, but blessings that build up the church with wonder, gratitude, and fidelity.

Theological knowledge, therefore, should not be treated as an end, but as a means to an end. Paul's prayer for the believers in Colossae makes this clear:

> For this reason, also, since the day we heard this, we have not stopped praying for you. We are asking that you may be filled with the knowledge of his will in all wisdom and spiritual understanding, so that you may walk worthy of the Lord, in order to please him in every way, bearing fruit in every good work and growing in the intimate way you know God. May you

---

[9] Fee, *The First Epistle to the Corinthians*, 368–69.

[10] 1 Corinthians 2:2.

[11] 1 Corinthians 3:16.

[12] 1 Corinthians 6:19.

Theology

be strengthened with power, according to his glorious might, for all endurance and patience, with joy giving thanks to the Father, who has enabled you to share in the saints' inheritance in the light.[13]

Paul prays that believers will have knowledge for a specific purpose: "so that [they] may walk worthy of the Lord." The technical theological term for this is orthopraxy. But orthopraxy is not the ultimate purpose. That is just a necessary step in the right direction. The ultimate end of knowledge is to "please [God] in every way."

Notice that Paul uses four participial phrases to describe the life that pleases God: 1) bearing fruit in every good work, 2) growing in an intimate personal relationship with God, 3) being empowered to endure adversity, and 4) expressing gratitude. Nowhere does Paul pray for anyone to have theological knowledge so that he or she can be the smartest person in the room and win every argument.

Theology should not be regarded as an academic endeavor for credentialed professionals. Theology must be developed, refined, tested, and applied in communities of faith, where Jesus' people "rejoice with those who rejoice, and weep with those who weep."[14] That context keeps theology grounded in reality. In our communities, as we do theology together, we can remind each other that theology is risky business because God is God, and we are what we are: rebellious, broken, and finite.

Our theology, therefore, will not be perfect (and that is an understatement). None of us are right about everything, which

---

[13] Colossians 1:9–12.
[14] Romans 12:15.

means that all of us are wrong about something, and most of us probably are wrong about many things.[15] Moreover, we may be technically right about certain theological points or issues, but still be wrong in the way we act about being right. If we can remember that theology is risky business, then we may avoid being arrogant, contentious, annoying people who do not know what we ought to know.

John Stott, a pastor who served in the same church for over thirty years, is one of my favorite theologians. Whenever I am reading anything by Stott, I know that I am catching a glimpse into the heart of a theologian who is not puffed up. In his commentary on Romans, Stott offers these observations about theology and doxology:

> It is important to note from Roman 1–11 that theology (our belief about God) and doxology (our worship of God) should never be separated. On the one hand, there can be no doxology without theology. It is not possible to worship an unknown god. All true worship is a response to the self-revelation of God in Christ and Scripture and arises from our reflection on who he is and what he has done. It was the tremendous truth of Roman 1–11 which provoked Paul's outburst of praise in verses 33–36 of chapter 11. The worship of God is evoked, informed and inspired by the vision of God. Worship without theology is bound to degenerate into idolatry. Hence the indispensable place of Scripture in

---

[15] John Polkinghorne offers this humble assessment of his own theological writing: "Karl Barth, arguably the greatest theologian of the twentieth century, once said that the angels would laugh when they read his theology. If they deign to read these pages, they will no doubt be in hysterics" (Polkinghorne, *Exploring Reality*, 178).

both public worship and private devotion. It is the word of God which calls forth the worship of God.

On the other hand, there should be no theology without doxology. There is something fundamentally flawed by the purely academic interest in God. That is not an appropriate object for cool, critical, detached, scientific observation and evaluation. No, the true knowledge of God will always lead us to worship, as it did Paul. Our place is on our faces before him in adoration.[16]

This is the impact of sound theology. It produces lives that are characterized by humility, gratitude, doxology, and love, lives that please God. This is the ultimate test of orthodoxy.

Lord, we confess that our theology misses the mark. Show us where our theology is wrong, and show us where our theology is right but our attitudes are wrong. Forgive us, and keep us from arrogance.

---

[16] Stott, *Romans*, 311.

CHAPTER 3

HISTORY

The kingdom of God is for everybody, but many people are not for the kingdom of God.

Often in Scripture the Greek word *christos* is used. Its literal meaning is "anointed one" and it is usually translated as "messiah." One dimension of the messianic expectation during the Second Temple period was that God would send a king to liberate his people and to establish his kingdom of shalom and justice.[1] That is why, in particular contexts, *The Voice*, a newer translation, translates *christos* as "God's Anointed, the Liberating King," I concur with that interpretation and use it often, as it captures that particular essence of Jesus' role in our lives. At the birth of the Messiah—God's Anointed, the Liberating King—the angel said: "Don't be afraid. I announce to you good news of great joy

---

[1] Bruce, *New Testament Development of Old Testament Themes*, 75; N. T. Wright, *Paul*, 42–43.

which will be for *all* people."[2] Of course, the angel was right. Jesus launched his movement with a startling announcement and an open invitation: "The time is now. The kingdom of God is at hand. Repent and believe the good news."[3] The good news was that the Kingdom was present because the King was present. All kinds of people responded to Jesus' gracious invitation: men and women; Samaritans, Jews, and Gentiles; notorious sinners and synagogue leaders; tax collectors and revolutionaries; hapless fishermen and prosperous land owners.

King Jesus secured the victory of his kingdom by humbling himself "to the point of death"[4] on a Roman cross, where he disarmed the hostile powers[5] by giving himself as "a ransom for all."[6] The resurrected and glorified Jesus, who will always be known as "the Lamb who was slaughtered,"[7] is worshiped in heaven as the "Savior of everyone"[8] whose kingdom includes "a vast multitude from every tribe and language and people and nation."[9] The inclusive nature of God's kingdom cannot be denied.

Yes, the Kingdom is for everybody ... but many people are not for the Kingdom. Who are the people who are not for the Kingdom? Jesus gives us a strong clue in the first line of his Kingdom Manifesto, generally known as the Sermon on the Mount: "Blessed are the poor in spirit, for theirs is the kingdom of

---

[2] Luke 2:10.
[3] Mark 1:15.
[4] Philippians 2:9.
[5] Colossians 2:15.
[6] 1 Timothy 2:6.
[7] Revelation 5:12.
[8] 1 Timothy 4:10.
[9] Revelation 5:9.

heaven."[10] If the kingdom of heaven belongs to the poor in spirit, then it seems reasonable to postulate that the people who are not poor in spirit are the people who are not for the kingdom of God. It is essential, therefore, to understand what it means to be poor in spirit.

The language of the New Testament has two words that mean *poor*. One word refers to the working poor, those who are able to subsist on what they earn, but have nothing extra.[11] The other word refers to those who are truly destitute, who cannot survive by their own labor or industry, but only by the charity of others.[12] This is the word that is used in the first beatitude, which may be translated: "Blessed are the destitute in spirit, for theirs is the kingdom of heaven."

The first beatitude forces us to ask some hard questions. Are we destitute in spirit? Have we abandoned all delusions of self-sufficiency and surrendered unconditionally to the grace of the Liberating King? Or does our vestigial, irrational pride persist? In spite of overwhelming evidence to the contrary, do we somehow manage to see ourselves as people who are able to enter, obtain, or establish God's kingdom by our own resources?

These are big questions. We know how we ought to answer them as a matter of theological correctness, but do we actually believe that we are utterly destitute in spirit? Are we truly humble? The stakes could not be higher. Jesus' words are all too clear. If we are destitute in spirit, then the Kingdom is for us. But

---

[10] Matthew 5:2.
[11] Morris, *The Gospel According to Matthew*, 95.
[12] Ibid.

if we are not destitute in spirit, we are not for the Kingdom. This is the cosmic divide.

In modern political discourse, ideological adversaries often accuse each other of being "on the wrong side of history."[13] Those who make such accusations typically fail to understand that history ultimately is not about the rise and fall of empires and political systems. In fact, those who claim to have deduced or induced the so-called right and wrong sides of history by the "normal resources of human insight"[14] display the type of arrogance that betrays their misunderstanding of the meaningfulness of history. Similarly, those who reject the idea that history has a right side or a wrong side, and dogmatically assert—based on the so-called verities of Science—that history has no meaning or purpose also are blinded by arrogance.[15]

From the first vision in Revelation, we learn that the meaning of history is not determined by brute force, political expedience, or philosophical inquiries. Rather, the meaning of history is found in the Kingdom that irrupts through the humility of the Lamb who was slaughtered, for only he is "worthy to open the scroll" that puts history in perspective.[16] The right and wrong sides of history are determined by God.

---

[13] See Daily Kos, August 8, 2010, "President Obama is on the Wrong Side of History" (www.dailykos.com), lamenting President Obama's then-opposition to same-sex marriage; see also Huffington Post, March 30, 2010, "Republicans on the Wrong Side of History" (www.huffingtonpost.com/barbrastreisand), criticizing opponents of President Obama's health care reform bill.

[14] Yoder, *The Politics of Jesus*, 232.

[15] Polkinghorne, *Belief in God in an Age of Science*, 12.

[16] Revelation 5:5–6.

John Howard Yoder offers this insight regarding the meaning of history:

> God's true purpose was the creation of a new society, unidentifiable with any of the local, national, or ethnic solidarities of any time. This new body, the church, as aftertaste of God's loving triumph on the cross and foretaste of His ultimate loving triumph in His kingdom, has a task within history. History is the framework in which the church evangelizes, so that the true meaning of history is the fact that God has chosen to use it for such a "scaffolding" service.[17]

The "new society" is populated by those who have responded to the gracious call of the crucified Messiah, and have joined him in the mission to proclaim the good news that God is making all things new. Only the humble, the destitute in spirit, are qualified for this mission because "God opposes the proud, but gives grace to the humble."[18]

Reinhold Niebuhr makes essentially the same point regarding the "eternal significance of [our] historical existence":

> The Christian hope of the consummation of life and history is less absurd than alternate doctrines which seek to comprehend the completion of life by some power or capacity inherent in man and his history. It is an integral part of the biblical conception of the meaning of life. Both the meaning and its fulfillment are ascribed to a centre and source beyond ourselves. We can participate in the meaning only if we do not seek too proudly

---

[17] Yoder, *The Christian Witness to the State*, 10–11.
[18] James 4:6.

to appropriate the meaning as our secure possession or to effect the fulfillment by our own power.[19]

The choice is clear but it is not easy. Lord, destroy our delusions that we can do anything without you. Show us that we are destitute in spirit so we can participate in your mission to make all things new. Amen.

---

[19] Niebuhr, "History as 'Finis' and 'Telos,'" 514.

CHAPTER 4

INTEGRITY

Recently, I had lunch with a new friend. As a relatively young man, he had reached the pinnacle of his profession; he had been a megachurch pastor. He was a gifted preacher. His church had 13,000 members. His sermons were televised. He was a rising star, but his heart was divided. He preached about integrity, but he did not live with integrity, and the truth came out. The news of his fall was covered by the media. He lost his family, his job, and his reputation. Finally, he lost his pride.

That was years ago. As he told his story, I was trying to picture him as he had been at the height of his powers, when he exuded confidence, when he seemed destined for so-called greatness. I was trying to imagine what his life must have been like when he was leading a huge congregation, preaching to thousands of people, yet living a double life. But I could not picture him as anything other than a humble brother, chastened by his past, surviving by grace, seeking wholeness, serving quietly. He may or may not ever preach another sermon about integrity, but he is living out God's plan: integrity through humility. You see, God has a cosmic agenda: shalom through love. And as part of his cosmic agenda, God has a personal agenda for each one of his children: integrity through humility.

Shalom is a Hebrew word that defies translation. In many contexts, shalom is translated as *peace*. That is a good start, but our conception of peace has been compromised and cheapened by the way things are in our rebellious and broken bogus world system. We typically use the word *peace* to describe a temporary respite from overt hostilities, a cease-fire, or a tenuous truce. That is not shalom. Caesar Augustus and his apologists used the word *peace* to describe the relative social tranquility and stability that Rome, under Augustus, imposed throughout the empire by the violence of the sword and the terror of the cross. The *Pax Romana* was a significant achievement, but it was not shalom.

Shalom requires justice. Shalom connotes ultimate and sustainable wholeness, wellness, and completeness.[1] Shalom means beauty, in the purest and deepest sense of that word.[2] God's good creation was characterized by shalom, but the shalom of Creation has been vandalized.[3] The creatures crafted in God's image have been "fractured from the Fall."[4] God's agenda in, through, and beyond history is to restore shalom, to make all things new, to replace the brokenness of the bogus world system with the beauty of the unshakable Kingdom.[5] God, however, does not impose his agenda through coercive power. Instead, shalom breaks into the

---

[1] Platinga, *Not the Way It's Supposed to Be*, 10.
[2] Seay, *The Gospel According to Jesus*, 156.
[3] Platinga, *Not the Way It's Supposed to Be*, 9–27.
[4] I borrowed this phrase from the Ryan Adams's song, "Two."
[5] Revelation 21; Hebrews 12:28.

broken world through humility and suffering love on a Roman cross. This is God's new creation project.

By grace, we are called and equipped to participate in this project. As the community of the Liberating King, we are part of the new creation.[6] Shalom—as God's gift and God's goal—should characterize our life together. On an individual level, shalom—as gift and goal—is "brought into focus through the word *integrity*," defined as the state of being whole, undivided, and sound.[7]

In our culture, a popular understanding of integrity is "practicing what you preach" and "walking your talk." This basic congruence between words and actions is commendable, and all too rare, but there is more to integrity. According to Scripture, integrity starts with and flows from an undivided or pure heart.

Consider, for example, the Ten Commandments, the covenant stipulations given by YHWH to Israel on stone tablets. In his introduction to the Ten Commandments, the Ibn Ezra[8] observed that "the commandments can be reduced to three categories: precepts of the heart (thought), precepts of the tongue (speech) and precepts of the hand (doing)."[9] In other words, the commandments require full integration and alignment of our thoughts, words, and actions. The Ibn Ezra continues: "The precepts of the heart are the most important of all . . . Many, however, imagine

---

[6] 2 Corinthians 5:17.

[7] Chuck De Groat, "a heart divided—the myth of 'Just be Yourself'" (www.drchuckdegroat.com).

[8] Abraham ibn Ezra was a Jewish scholar (mathematician, philosopher, poet, exegete) who lived in the Middle Ages.

[9] Abraham ibn Ezra, *Abraham ibn Ezra's Commentary to the Pentateuch* (quoted in "Exodus 20—The Ten Commandments and 4 More Chiastic Structures," Thinking Tanakh, at tanakh.blogspur.com).

that thinking idolatry (for example) is no crime whereas this is much worse than any other . . . The first commandment is the most important principle that underlies the remaining nine."[10]

The Ibn Ezra is right. If my heart is divided, if I am "thinking idolatry," serving any god(s) other than the one true God, then I will not be whole, undivided, and sound. That is why the *Shema Yisrael* is one of the foundational confessions and prayers of the Hebrew Scriptures: "Hear, O Israel! YHWH is our God, YHWH alone. And you must love YHWH your God with all your heart, all your soul, and all your strength."[11] Integrity starts with the heart's undivided allegiance to the one true God.

The Ten Commandments point to integrity, but they cannot produce integrity because the human heart has been corrupted, hardened, and divided by sin. That is why God's new creation project begins with the promise of a new heart: "I will give them singleness of heart, and put a new Spirit in them. I will take away their hearts of stone and give them tender hearts instead so they will obey my laws and regulations."[12] Under the Old Covenant, the law was "chiseled on stone tablets."[13] Under the New Covenant, inaugurated and secured by the broken body and shed blood of Jesus, the law is written by God's Spirit on new hearts.[14] The letter of the law could not produce integrity, but the Spirit can and does.

What does integrity look like in the bogus world system? Jesus is our exemplar, the prototype:

---

[10] Ibid.
[11] Deuteronomy 6:4.
[12] Ezekiel 37:26.
[13] 2 Corinthians 3:3.
[14] Jeremiah 31:30—34; 2 Corinthians 3:3.

> For you were called to this,
> Because the Liberating King suffered for you,
> Leaving you an example,
> So that you should follow in his steps.
> "He did not sin,
> And he did not lie";
> When slandered, he did not slander in return;
> When suffering, he did not threaten,
> But entrusted himself completely to the One who judges with justice.[15]

The integrity of Jesus started with his undivided heart. He committed himself completely to the Father, praying "not my will, but yours, be done."[16] Because of that heart commitment, he had integrity in his speech (he did not lie or slander) and in his actions (he did not sin). Jesus' integrity makes our integrity possible: "My wholeness, my integrity, is made possible by the truthfulness of the story [of Jesus]. Through the story of Jesus I can increasingly learn to be what I have become, a participant in God's community of peace and justice."[17]

In his teaching, Jesus commended the "pure in heart" whose "righteousness surpasses that of the scribes and Pharisees."[18] The scribes and Pharisees focused on—and took pride in—technical compliance with the commandments (for example, do not murder, do not commit adultery). Jesus warned about infractions of the

---

[15] 1 Peter 2:21–23.

[16] Luke 22:42.

[17] Hauerwas, *The Hauerwas Reader*, 14.

[18] Matthew 5:8, 20.

heart (for example, anger, lust),[19] and—when his disciples were accused of violating the law by eating with unwashed hands—Jesus countered that "eating with unwashed hands does not defile a person," but "what comes out of the mouth comes from the heart and that is what defiles a person."[20]

The scribes and Pharisees "practiced their righteousness in front of people to be seen by them," but their hearts were "full of greed and self-indulgence."[21] Jesus calls his followers to cultivate a "secret" righteousness that only God can see.[22] Therefore, in sharp contrast to the ways of the bogus world system, where "perception is reality" and "image is everything," where we try to hide our lust, fear, and enmity under a veneer of respectable propriety and civility, Jesus calls us to cultivate hidden lives that are *better* than the good works that people see! This is Jesus-style integrity.

Paul, the "apostle of the heart set free,"[23] understood Jesus-style integrity. He wrote to his contentious and image-conscious friends in Corinth: "We have renounced shameful secret things, not walking in deceit or distorting God's message, but in God's sight we commend ourselves to every person's conscience by an open display of the truth."[24] Instead of investing his energy in what people could see, Paul focused on the Spirit's renewing work in his "inner person," his heart.[25]

---

[19] Matthew 5:21–30.

[20] Mark 7:20.

[21] Matthew 6:1; 23:25.

[22] Matthew 6: 1–18.

[23] This phrase is taken from the title to a classic introduction to Paul and his theology by F. F. Bruce—*Paul: Apostle of the Heart Set Free*.

[24] 2 Corinthians 4:2.

[25] 2 Corinthians 4:15.

How do we become people of integrity? The first step is to face reality with humility: we are fractured, and our hearts are broken and divided. The second step is to pray (and keep praying) a broken-hearted prayer of consecration. Julie Miller's song "Broken Things" is a beautiful example:

> You can have my heart
> if you don't mind broken things.
> You can have my life
> if you don't mind these tears.
> Well I heard that you make all things new
> So I give the pieces all to you
> If you want it you can have my heart.[26]

The third step is to focus on the renewal of the inner person, the righteousness of the hidden life, so that the "just requirements of the law (may) be accomplished in us who do not walk according to our own resources but according to the Spirit."[27] Each step requires humility.

Pope Benedict XVI describes the path to integrity as following Jesus "in the descent of humble service":

> Purification of heart occurs as a consequence of following Christ, of becoming one with him. "It is no longer I who live, but Christ lives in me" (Gal. 2:20). And at this point, something new comes to light: The ascent to God occurs precisely in the descent of humble service, in the descent of love, for love is God's essence, and is thus the power that truly purifies man and enables him

---

[26] Julie Miller, "Broken Things," *Broken Things* (Hightone, 1999).
[27] Romans 8:2.

to see him. In Jesus Christ, God has revealed himself in his descending... to the point of death on the Cross. And precisely by doing so, he reveals himself in his true divinity. We ascend to God by accompanying him on his descending path... The pure heart is the loving heart that enters into communion of service and obedience with Jesus Christ. Love is the fire that purifies and unifies intellect, will, and emotion, thereby making man one with himself, inasmuch as it makes him one in God's eyes.[28]

Father, we pray for the shalom and integrity of your kingdom. We surrender our broken and divided hearts to you. Holy Spirit, give us Jesus-style integrity, seasoned with humility. Make us people who do what we say, and say what we think, and have the mind and heart of the Liberating King. Amen.

---

[28] Ratzinger, *Jesus of Nazareth: From the Baptism in the Jordan to the Transfiguration*, 95–96.

CHAPTER 5

INDUSTRY

The Puritan Work Ethic theory (PWE) posits a causal nexus between Calvinism and vocational diligence or industriousness. Some social scientists have argued that the Calvinist doctrine of election creates personal anxiety and uncertainty, which causes Calvinists to work with diligence and discipline to prove that they are among the elect.[1]

There are several problems with this argument. First, it misreads or misunderstands the spiritual dynamics of Calvinism to the extent it assumes or postulates that Calvinists tend to be beset by anxiety and uncertainty. Second, it fails to account for the exemplary work ethic of non-Calvinists. For example, the Amish do not subscribe to the Calvinist doctrine of election, but they are noted for hard work and discipline, as are participants

---

[1] German sociologist Max Weber advanced the PWE theory in *The Protestant Ethic and the Spirit of Capitalism*. The book was first published in English in 1930.

Industry

in Catholic religious orders. Third, I personally know a bunch of young Calvinists who seem to be complete slackers. They mostly sit around drinking coffee, blogging about supralapsarianism, and pondering whether their next tattoo should be a portrait of Jonathan Edwards or John Owen.

Notwithstanding the viability of the PWE as a socioeconomic theory, there *should* be a correlation between Christian faith and industriousness because Scripture consistently condemns laziness and commends hard work.[2] Even so, the church—as a community marked by generosity and grace—has been a magnet for freeloaders and slackers since the first century. For example, in Thessalonica, some people who could work chose not to work. Apparently, they were happy to live off of the work of others. Paul, the tentmaker who labored at his trade day and night so that he would not be a burden to others,[3] could not let this go:

> About brotherly love: you don't need me to write you because you yourselves are taught by God to love one another. In fact, you are doing this toward all the brothers and sisters in the entire region of Macedonia. We encourage you, brothers and sisters, to do even more, to seek to lead a quiet life, to mind your own business and to work with your own hands, as we commanded you, so that you may walk properly in the presence of outsiders and not be dependent on anyone.[4]

Paul frames the issue as a matter of mutual love and respect. Those who are able to work should work so that 1) they will not

---

[2] See, e.g., Proverbs 6:6–11, 10:4, 12:7, 19:15, 26:13–16.
[3] 1 Thessalonians 2:9.
[4] 1 Thessalonians 4:9–12.

intrude on their brothers and sisters by becoming a burden, 2) they will be able to take care of their own needs, and 3) they will be effective witnesses to those who are outside the church. Although Paul does not explicitly talk about pride and humility in this context, it is clear that the directive to work is a matter of putting the interests of others ahead of self-interest, a mark of true humility. That is why and how Paul worked, and that is why and how he expected Jesus' followers to work.

Paul's gentle admonition may have been too subtle. Some of the slackers did not get the message. In a subsequent letter to the same church, Paul tackles the problem again:

> Now we command you, brothers and sisters, in the name of our Lord Jesus, the Liberating King, to keep away from every brother and sister who walks irresponsibly and not according to the tradition received from us. For you yourselves know how you must imitate us: we were not irresponsible among you. We did not eat anyone's bread free of charge; instead, we labored and toiled, working night and day, so that we would not be a burden to any of you. It is not that we don't have the right to support, but we did it to make ourselves an example to you so that you would imitate us. In fact, when we were with you, this is what we commanded you: "If anyone isn't willing to work, he should not eat." For we hear that there are some among you who walk irresponsibly, not working at all, but interfering with the work of others. Now we command and exhort such people, by the Lord Jesus, the Liberating King, that quietly working, they may eat their own bread. Brothers and sisters, do not grow weary in doing good.[5]

---

[5] 2 Thessalonians 3:6–13.

Industry

In this passage, it is clear that the slackers are disruptive to the shalom of the community. It would be bad enough if they simply refused to work, but they also were interfering with or disrupting the work of others. In response, Paul imposes the ultimate New Testament sanction: disassociation. There are no more "free lunches" for the disruptive slackers. A term and condition of continued or restored fellowship is the willingness to work and contribute. This action is taken to protect the community, but it is also designed to be redemptive. Paul hopes that the disruptive slackers will be humbled into doing the right thing.

How do these principles apply to the contemporary American church? The first principle is clear. Everything we do should be motivated by love for our brothers and sisters. If we appropriate a "rule" (e.g., you can't eat if you aren't willing to work), but we don't show love, we are missing the mark. In love, however, we should not enable slackers to be slackers; rather, we should encourage them to work because "idleness [is] the enemy of the soul."[6]

Some may object that they don't want to be stuck with a boring "straight" job because they have a "passion" for ministry—or art or music or fishing or some other noble, non-mundane endeavor. This passion-based objection can be a pretext for pride, particularly if someone feels that he is too good, smart, or talented for most available jobs. This objection must be rejected because the best training in humility is doing a "lowly" job "enthusiastically, as something done for the Lord, and not for men."[7] When we do this, any workplace can be a place where the kingdom of God breaks in.

---

[6] Rule of Saint Francis of Assisi, § V.
[7] Colossians 3:23.

One of the sad and ironic consequences of not working is not truly resting. There is no rest without work. God worked six days, and on the seventh day he did not work.[8] God commanded Israel to labor for six days, "but the seventh day is a Sabbath of YHWH your God; [on that day] you shall not do any work."[9] The command to rest is predicated on the prior command to work, and both commands are predicated on God's example. God intended this pattern of work and rest to be a gift and a blessing for his people, but the religious regulators managed to turn the Sabbath into an intolerable, dehumanizing burden. They developed an elaborate set of rules (sometimes called hedging restrictions) to avoid any possibility of infringing the Sabbath; then they became proud of their strict technical compliance with their own rules.[10] On several occasions, the Pharisees actually had the audacity to challenge Jesus for his alleged violations of the Sabbath rules.[11] Jesus, the Lord of the Sabbath, dismissed their allegations, and reminded them of an incontrovertible biblical fact: "The Sabbath was made for people, not people for the Sabbath."[12] But we will never enjoy the blessing of a Sabbath if we fail or refuse to find the blessing of work.

If you have been reading this chapter with a sense of satisfaction based on your personal drive and industriousness, then your humility may still need some work as you may be prone to another type of pride: the pride that infects highly motivated entrepreneurs. In sharp contrast to the slackers, who may be too

---

[8] Genesis 2:2–3.
[9] Genesis 20:8–11.
[10] Cole, *Mark*, 129.
[11] Bock, *Jesus According to Scripture*, 607–9.
[12] Mark 2:27–28.

Industry

proud to work, entrepreneurs may too proud of their commercial endeavors. James has a strong word for these folks:

> Come now, you who say, "today or tomorrow we will travel to such and such a city and spend a year there and do business and make a profit." You don't even know what tomorrow will bring—what your life will be! For you are a bit of smoke that appears for a little while, then vanishes. Instead, you should say, "if the Lord wills, we will live and do this or that." But as it is, you boast in your arrogance. All such boasting is evil.[13]

James is chastising those who make big plans based on the dubious presumption that they know what tomorrow will bring. The problem is not the idea of planning, or the desire to make a profit, the problem is the arrogant approach to the enterprise. The starting point for each and every plan should be a prayer of unconditional surrender and trust ("Father, not my will, but yours be done"[14]) and a humble request for wisdom.[15]

I write as one who has wrestled with and been chastened by James' warning to entrepreneurs. I have been blessed to be part of a growing and thriving law firm. My law partners and I try to run our law firm with the proper mix of fidelity and humility, but we often miss the mark. Sometimes we make bold plans based on dubious presumptions, and God graciously allows us to see the futility and foolishness of autonomous commercial endeavors. Sometimes we are tempted to boast about our success, but God graciously reminds us that the law firm is his business, that he has

---

[13] James 4:13–16.
[14] Luke 22:42.
[15] James 1:5.

been pleased to bless us for his purposes, and that the only true measure of success is faithfulness to him.

Lord, we thank you for the way you work in our lives through our work. Keep us from being proud slackers, and also keep us from being proud producers. Forgive us for dubious presumptions. We submit our working lives to your will, and we humbly ask for your wisdom. Amen.

CHAPTER 6

PROSPERITY

I first heard the good news about Jesus in a Young Life meeting in October of 1972. I now have been involved in Young Life in one way or another for more than forty years. Over the course of several decades of marriage, as Young Life leaders, Diana and I have been privileged "to share not only the gospel of God, but our lives as well"[1] with many young people, most of whom are not so young today. A few years ago, I had the following conversation with a young man, a high school senior who had been hanging around our house for months:

Chris: What do you do?

Me: What do you mean? I do a lot of things.

Chris: I mean for money. Do you have a job or something?

Me: Yes.

---
[1] 1 Thessalonians 2:8.

Chris:	I heard you are a lawyer. Is that true?
Me:	Indeed, I am a lawyer.
Chris:	I did not believe that when I heard it. You must not be a very good lawyer.
Me:	Uhh.
Chris:	I mean, I have seen where the good lawyers live, what they drive . . .
Me:	Uhh.
Chris:	. . . it just seems that you must not be a very good lawyer.
Me:	Do you want to arm wrestle?

I felt a strong urge to set this kid straight. I wanted to tell him about my professional credentials, my impressive litany of accolades, my role as managing partner of a successful law firm, my highly-coveted corner office, my high-profile clients, my notable victories . . . but I decided to let it go. I had no response.

In that moment, I was double-crossed by my multifaceted pride. On the one hand, I realized that I was proud of my professional success, and I wanted Chris to understand that he was dealing with a bona fide big shot. On the other hand, I realized that I was equally proud of my relatively simple lifestyle, and I could not wait to talk about my conversation with Chris in order to impress other Christians with my piety. Oh, brother. The first type of pride is the garden-variety pride of the "successful" person in the bogus world system. That is the subject of this chapter. The second type of pride—religious pride—is even more pernicious. That is the subject of the next chapter.

Prosperity

The New Testament does not outlaw prosperity or prohibit financial success. The New Testament does, however, offer some very strong warnings about the "deceitfulness of wealth."[2] Consider, for example, Paul's words to Timothy:

> Here's what you say to those wealthy in regard to this age: "Don't become high and mighty or place all your hope on a gamble for riches; instead, fix your hope on God, the One who richly provides everything for our enjoyment." Tell them to use their wealth for good things; be rich in good works! If they are willing to give generously and share everything, then they will send ahead a great treasure for themselves and build their futures on a solid foundation. As a result, they will surely take hold of eternal life.[3]

In this passage, Paul makes several salient points. First, wealth has a tendency to produce arrogance.[4] If I think that I am wealthy because I am better than you, and/or if I think that I am better than you because I am wealthy, then I am an arrogant person ... and an ignorant person. I am disconnected from reality because I have failed to understand that all that I have—including "my stuff" and the talents and opportunities that have allowed me

---

[2] Mark 4:19.

[3] 1 Timothy 6:17–19 (*The Voice*).

[4] I recommend two cautionary case studies on the relationship between wealth and arrogance. The first is the King of Tyre, whose heart was proud because of his riches (Ezekiel 28:5). He actually claimed to be a god (Ezekiel 28:2). He was mistaken. The second is the Wall Street trader in Tom Wolfe's novel, *The Bonfire of the Vanities*. Based on his commissions from zero-coupon bonds, he thought he was a "Master of the Universe." He, too, was mistaken.

to get that stuff—belongs to God. He is the ultimate owner and provider of everything.[5]

In that arrogance, I also am ignorant about the reality of my spiritual bankruptcy. This is precisely the situation that prompted Jesus to rebuke the church in Laodicea: "You say, 'I am rich; I have become wealthy, and need nothing,' [but] you don't know you are wretched, pitiful, poor, blind, and naked."[6]

Second, material wealth is uncertain, a gamble. Jesus made this point when he warned us not to "treasure up for ourselves treasures on earth where moth and rust destroy and where thieves break in and steal."[7] Jesus is not against us accumulating treasures for ourselves. He is simply warning us about the inherently risky nature of the earthly treasury. That is why he tells us to "treasure up treasures for ourselves" in his kingdom, "where neither moth nor rust destroys, and thieves don't break in and steal."[8]

Third, wealth is a bogus god. Jesus warns us that it is absolutely impossible to serve God and the spiritual power known as Mammon.[9] Jacques Ellul urges us to take this warning seriously:

> We absolutely must not minimize the parallel Jesus draws between God and Mammon. He is not using a rhetorical figure

---

[5] 1 Timothy 6:17; Psalm 24:1. In Deuteronomy, Moses predicts that, once God's people taste the abundance of the promised land, they will be tempted to say that they became wealthy by their own power and strength (8:17). They are commanded to remember YHWH, "for it is he who gives you the power to make wealth" (8:18).

[6] Revelation 3:17.

[7] Matthew 6:19.

[8] Matthew 6:21.

[9] Matthew 6:24.

but pointing out a reality. God as a person and Mammon as a person find themselves in conflict. Jesus describes the relation between us and one or the other the same way: it is the relationship between servant and master. Mammon can be a master the same way God is; that is, Mammon can be a personal master.[10]

Mammon demands our love and our trust, but he "rewards" us only with a deadly mix of pride, greed, and anxiety. By definition, therefore, Mammon is a lousy god. That is why the psalmist points out the foolishness of "the man who would not make God his refuge, but trusted in the abundance of his riches."[11] Our hope must be set completely on the one true God.[12] We are not called to have a diversified hope portfolio—our hope must only be in Christ.

Fourth, we who are wealthy must be radically "generous, willing to share."[13] Ellul calls Christian giving a liberating act of profanation:

> The ultimate expression of this Christian attitude toward the power of money is what we will call *profanation*. To profane money, like all other powers, is to take away its sacred character. For although we usually think of profaning goods or values that are religious in the positive sense, it is just as possible to conduct such an assault against Satan and all he inspires ... There is one act par excellence which profanes money by going directly

---

[10] Ellul, *Money & Power*, 76.
[11] Psalm 52:7.
[12] 1 Peter 1:13.
[13] 1 Timothy 6:18.

against the law of money, an act for which money is not made. This act is *giving*.[14]

The act of giving is the only way to avoid the "temptation and trap" posed by the "love of money."[15] This misplaced affection is spiritually ruinous. Some, by craving money, "have wandered away from the faith."[16] Jesus makes this same point in the parable of the sower and the seed, when he describes the plight of the seed that fell among the thorns: "The worries of the bogus world system and the pleasures of wealth choke the word and it becomes unfruitful."[17]

Jesus' parable of the "rich fool"[18] illustrates all of these important points. The rich fool, after being blessed with a good crop, built bigger barns to store his abundance so he could "take life easy."[19] The plan did not end well because he stored up things for himself, but "was not rich towards God."[20]

The fact is that we were created for a whole lot more than the bogus world system can offer. Todd Snider captures this perfectly in an Americana gospel song:

> Some guys are looking for diamonds
> Some guys just want to pay their bills
> Some guys are climbing up mountains

---

[14] Ellul, *Money & Power*, 109–10.
[15] 1 Timothy 6:9–10.
[16] Ibid.
[17] Matthew 13:22.
[18] Luke 12:16–21.
[19] Luke 12:19.
[20] Luke 12:21.

Prosperity

While others are digging for thrills
Some guys just want to win trophies
Some guys just want to get girls
Some guys swear they won't stop working
Until they own everything in the world.

Well good luck at the end of that rainbow
If you think that's what you're here for
But make no mistake about it, Baby
I want a whole lot more
I want a whole lot more.

Sometimes I see people out here
Playing every single one of their cards
For bigger this or better that
Or greener grass 'round the pools in their yard
They work and they slave
Just so they can save
Up a whole lot to leave behind
Some guys are just so certain success
Is the key to their peace of mind.

I want a whole lot more than treasures
That I can store down here on Earth.
Price them any way you want to.
Hey, buddy, I know what they're worth.

Yes, some guys want attention, some guys want
   girls
And some dig kicking down doors

> Some guys want everything in this whole wide world
> I want a whole lot more
> I want a whole lot more.[21]

You probably have heard about certain Pentecostals in the Deep South who demonstrate their faith by handling rattlesnakes, copperheads, and water moccasins in their worship services. As if that is not enough, some of them also drink poison. They base these colorful and distinctive practices on a passage that appears in Mark 16 of the King James Version. One problem, of course, is that we are 99 percent certain that the passage was not originally part of Mark's Gospel or any other canonical text; it was added later by a scribe.[22] These brothers and sisters are risking their lives based on a text that is not really in the Bible!

But we cannot point fingers at these snake-handling, poison-chugging brothers and sisters because many of us also engage in equally dangerous and misguided behavior. We casually dismiss the express warnings of Scripture about the dangers of wealth. We continue to entertain the destructive delusion that we can serve God and Mammon, and we ignore the needs of others as we set our minds on "everything in this whole wide world" when God is offering us "a whole lot more."

How can we avoid such dangerous behavior? Paul, writing from prison, gives the answer in Philippians 4. The chapter begins with several vital imperatives, and a transformative promise: 1) rejoice always, 2) don't worry about anything, 3) pray about

---

[21] Todd Snider, "A Lot More," *Songs from the Daily Planet* (Nashville: MCA, 1994).

[22] Cole, *Mark*, 334–35.

everything, and 4) God will give you shalom, the peace that is beyond human comprehension.[23] From there, Paul moves on to two more vital imperatives, and another transformative promise: 1) set your minds on all that is beautiful and true, 2) imitate Paul, who is imitating the cruciform pattern of Jesus, and 3) the God of shalom will be with you.[24] In light of those imperatives and promises, Paul thanks the Philippians for their support, and writes:

> I rejoiced in the Lord greatly that now at last you have renewed your care for me. You were, in fact, concerned about me, but you did not have the opportunity to show it. I don't say this because of need, for I have learned to be content in whatever circumstances I am. I know how to have a little, and I know how to have a lot. In any and all circumstances, I have learned the secret of contentment—whether well-fed or hungry, whether in abundance or in need. I am able to do all things through the One who strengthens me.[25]

The "secret" weapon in the struggle to resist the allure of Mammon is "contentment." The word translated as "contentment" has a rich history in Greek philosophy. For the Stoics, this word meant "self-sufficiency," the character trait that enabled a wise person to maintain perspective and dignity in all circumstances.[26] For Paul, the word means "Christ-sufficiency," the supra-rational shalom that comes from the personal presence of

---

[23] Philippians 4:4–7.
[24] Philippians 4:8–9.
[25] Philippians 4:10–13.
[26] Fee, *Paul's Letter to the Philippians*, 432–34.

the God of shalom.[27] This is the "secret" that must be "learned." Mammon cannot offer anything comparable.

Lord, help us to watch out for the deadly temptations of arrogance, anxiety, and idolatry. Jesus, keep us humble and grateful, protect us from the tempter, and give us the wisdom to treasure up treasures in your kingdom by imitating your radical generosity. Amen.

---

[27] Ibid., 434.

CHAPTER 7

RELIGIOSITY

As a police officer, I was trained to spot counterfeit money. That was not as much fun as practicing pursuit driving skills or learning a variety of chokeholds, but it was useful. The best way to identify bogus currency is to be thoroughly familiar with real currency. I am amazed at how people who handle money every day can and do fall for counterfeit money. For example, during the George W. Bush administration, a customer at a fast food establishment paid for $2.00 worth of food with a $200 bill. That should have been a clue, but it was not the only clue. The $200 bill featured a picture of George W. Bush, and was inscribed with the patriotic slogan "I like broccoli." The customer was given $198 in change.[1]

As followers of Jesus, we need to be able to spot bogus religiosity. In the Kingdom Manifesto (better known as the Sermon on the Mount), Jesus warned about false prophets and other posers,

---

[1] www.itsamoneything.com/trivia (citing a Reuters news story dated February 1, 2001).

but—through the centuries—Jesus' people have been continually tempted to accept a counterfeit version of the faith. That is why James gives us a clear description of authentic religion: "Pure and undefiled religion before our God and Father is this: to look after orphans and widows in their distress and to avoid the pollution of the bogus world system."[2]

When I first encountered this verse (out of context of course), I was puzzled by what James did not include in this succinct description of authentic religion. For example, the verse does not mention Jesus and/or faith. When the verse is read in context, it is clear that he expects and assumes his readers to understand that authentic religion begins with personal/communal "faith in our glorious Lord Jesus the Liberating King."[3] From that starting point, James argues that people who participate in this faith are not only "hearers" and "talkers," but "doers."[4] What do they do? In Jesus' name, they engage in practical acts of service to those who are in distress and have nothing to offer in return, and they avoid the "pollution" of the bogus world system.

How can Jesus' people avoid the pollution of this world? James answers that question in chapter 4. First, recognize that there can be no compromise or negotiated truce with the bogus world system, which is driven by "selfish ambition."[5] Second, since there can be no compromise or negotiated truce between the people of God and the world system, the only viable option is unconditional surrender (to God), which requires humility.[6]

---

[2] James 1:27.
[3] James 2:1.
[4] James 1:22–23.
[5] James 4:4; cf. James 3:14–16.
[6] James 4:7–10.

Religiosity

Once we are clear on the essential characteristics of authentic religion, we should be able to spot the practitioners of bogus religiosity. There are many traits and varieties of bogus religiosity. Here are a few:

1. It is often characterized by hypocrisy. One type of hypocrisy is to establish or advocate one set of rules, but to live by another set of rules.[7] A variation on that theme is to focus on strict hyper-technical compliance with selected rules and regulations relating to minutiae, but to ignore the "most important matters" such as "justice, mercy, and faith."[8] Another variation on the theme is to focus on externalities, the types of practices that people can see, without confronting the greed and self-indulgence that corrupts the heart.[9] Jesus condemned the Pharisees for all of these things, but these types of hypocrisy have persisted throughout the centuries, and are pervasive today.

2. Bogus religiosity often is characterized by showmanship. Jesus made fun of the religious showoffs who practice their version of righteousness "in front of people to be seen by them," by sounding a trumpet when they give to the poor, praying long fancy prayers on street corners, and by fasting with sad "hey-look-at-me-I'm-really-hungry" faces.[10] Jesus could not have been clearer on this topic, but religious showmanship has persisted throughout the centuries, and flourishes today.

3. Bogus religiosity often is characterized by a lack of self-control. James talks about the one who "thinks he is religious" but

---

[7] Matthew 23:3–4.
[8] Matthew 23:23.
[9] Matthew 23:5, 25–28.
[10] Matthew 6:1–18.

does not control his tongue."[11] Unlike the hypocrites and showoffs mentioned above, who try to (and often do) fool other people with their religiosity, James points out that the people who lack control are only fooling themselves, and their so-called religion is "useless."[12]

4. Finally, counterfeit religiosity often is characterized by dubious motives. For example, Paul warns the Corinthians about those "who peddle God's message for profit,"[13] and he warns Timothy about false teachers "who imagine that godliness is a way to material gain."[14] Jesus took extreme measures to deal with the rip-off artists who turned the temple into a "den of thieves."[15] Today, perhaps more than ever, the nefarious nexus between bogus religiosity and selfish opportunism continues to undermine or compromise the mission of the church.

The sine qua non of bogus religiosity is humility's enemy, pride, ironically often thinly disguised as false humility. For example, the religious regulators in Colossians were "inflated without cause," and they actually took pride in their so-called humility![16] The false humility of bogus religiosity was a problem in the days of Isaiah. The people were proud of their fasting, and they were frustrated by God's failure to be duly impressed. They asked God, "Why have we fasted and you do not see? Why have we humbled ourselves and you do not notice."[17] God responded

---

[11] James 1:26.
[12] Ibid.
[13] 2 Corinthians 2:17.
[14] 1 Timothy 6:5.
[15] Mark 16:15–18.
[16] Colossians 2:18.
[17] Isaiah 58:3.

through Isaiah, pointing out that their fasting was an empty religious exercise because they had no hunger for justice:

> What good is fasting when you keep on fighting and quarreling?
> This kind of fasting will never get you anywhere with me.
>
> You humble yourselves by going through the motions of penance,
> bowing your heads like reeds bending in the wind.
> You dress in burlap and cover yourselves with ashes.
> Is this what you call fasting?
> Do you really think this will please YHWH?[18]

The poster child for bogus religiosity is the proud Pharisee who prayed: "God, I thank you that I am not like the other people—greedy, unrighteous, adulterers, or even like this tax collector. I fast twice a week. I give a tenth of everything I get."[19]

I have never heard a real prayer quite as obnoxious as that one, but I know how religious pride infects our perspective. I suspect that there are some today who might be tempted to pray: "Lord I thank you that I am not like the other people—the ones who drink, smoke, and watch R-rated movies. I go to church twice a week, and I vote for conservative Republicans."

---

[18] Isaiah 58:4–5.
[19] Luke 18:11–12.

Some of my progressive brothers and sisters may be nodding in approval, but they are not immune to religious pride. They may be tempted to pray: "Lord, I thank you that I am not like those legalists—the ones who drive SUV's, live in the suburbs, poison their children with Happy Meals, and work for greedy corporations. I watch independent films, eat locally grown, organic food, drive a hybrid car (when I am not riding a bike), and blog about social justice."

Bogus religiosity should be easier to spot than "I like broccoli" Bush bucks. But we fall for it and fall into it all of the time. Notwithstanding its persistence and pervasiveness, there is no future in bogus religiosity. All of us must check ourselves for the religious pride that fuels bogus religiosity. All of us should humble ourselves and pray:

"Lord, have mercy on us, because we are sinners."

CHAPTER 8

CERTAINTY

In *Plan B: Further Thoughts on Faith*, Anne Lamott confidently declares: "The opposite of faith is not doubt, it is certainty. Certainty is missing the point entirely. Faith includes noticing the mess, the emptiness and discomfort, and letting it be there until some light comes."[1] The author of Hebrews does not seem to share Lamott's low view of certainty: "Faith celebrates the certainty [of the blessings] for which we hope, the evidence of events as yet unseen."[2]

Notwithstanding the express verbal contradiction (faith is the opposite of certainty vs. faith celebrates certainty), the two statements may be reconciled once the key terms are defined in their respective contexts. For Lamott, faith connotes living with authenticity, without pretension or denial, holding on to God in

---

[1] Lamott, *Plan B*, 256–57.

[2] Hebrews 11:1. This translation is based on the exegetical notes in William Lanes's commentary, *Hebrews 9–13*, 325–26.

the midst of "the mess." Certainty, therefore, as the opposite of faith, apparently arises from an ignoble combination of phoniness and arrogance, and produces dogmatism detached from and indifferent to reality, also known as "the mess."

For the author of Hebrews, faith means "steadfast faithfulness to God and his word of promise."[3] The word translated as "certainty" is *hypostasis*, which "designates an objective reality that is unquestionably and securely established."[4] The word translated as "evidence" is *elenchos*, in this context understood "in the objective sense of 'proof' or 'demonstration,' the evidential character that deprives uncertainty of any basis."[5] Faith "is thus an effective power directed toward the future"[6] (comprising hoped-for blessings and not-yet-seen-events) that materially alters life here and now.

> [Faith] springs from a direct, personal encounter with the living God. The forward-looking capacity of faith enables an individual to venture courageously and serenely into an unseen future, supported only by the word of God. As a positive orientation of life toward God and his word, faith has the capacity to unveil the future so that the solid reality of events yet unseen can be grasped by the believer.[7]

In Hebrews, faith celebrates the certainty that God will keep his promises, including the promise of ultimate and complete

---

[3] Lane, *Hebrews 9–13*, 328.
[4] Ibid.
[5] Ibid.
[6] Ibid., 329.
[7] Ibid.

Certainty

redemption in the "kingdom that cannot be shaken."[8] Faith, however, does not eliminate the uncertainties of day-to-day life in the bogus world system as we press on toward that Kingdom. Rather, faith allows us to persevere through the fog. The story of Abraham confirms that faith works in and through uncertainty:

> By faith Abraham, when he was called, obeyed by going out to a place which he was to receive as an inheritance; and he went out, not knowing where he was going. By faith he lived as an alien in the land of promise, as in a foreign land, dwelling in tents with Isaac and Jacob, fellow heirs of the same promise; for he was looking for the city whose architect and builder is God.[9]

If there were no uncertainties in life, there would be no need for faith. By definition true faith always requires an element of the unknown, since, after all, if everything was known, it wouldn't be faith, but merely an acknowledgment of fact. Phillip Yancey puts it this way: "Faith demands uncertainty, confusion."[10] But if we are uncertain about God's ability or willingness to keep his promises, we will not live by faith. And if we do not live by faith, we will not please God.[11] Therefore, just as there are two types of cholesterol (typically labeled as "good" and "bad"), there are two types of certainty. The certainty that is "the opposite of faith" is proud certainty; the person who has this type of certainty has misplaced

---

[8] Hebrews 12:28.
[9] Hebrews 11:8–10.
[10] Yancey, *Disappointment with God*, 236.
[11] Hebrews 11:6.

confidence in his own theological correctness, innate wisdom, moral rectitude, and intestinal fortitude. For the purposes of this essay, we will call this type of certainty "P-Certainty." The certainty that arises from and is celebrated by faith is humble certainty; the person who has this type of certainty puts "no confidence in the flesh."[12] His confidence is in God's faithfulness. For the purposes of this essay, we will call this type of certainty "H-Certainty."

The Bible provides several notable case studies on P-Certainty. For example, consider the friends of Job: Eliphaz, Bildad, and Shofar. These men came to Job when Job was reeling from a series of catastrophic losses. They spoke confidently into Job's pain with a frustrating mix of pious platitudes, untested truisms, religious banalities, and baseless accusations. "In short, Job's friends emerge as self-righteous dogmatists who defend the mysterious ways of God. Confident of their proper doctrine and sound arguments, they cast judgment on Job."[13] Their basic point: "Job, shut your piehole. Life is fair because God is just." Their speeches exemplify what Lamott means by "missing the point" and ignoring "the mess." The point of the Book of Job is that life in this broken world is not fair, nevertheless God is just.[14] At the end of Job, God rebukes Job's friends for their "folly" because they "have not spoken of [God] what is right."[15]

Another case study in P-Certainty is Peter. He was a confident man, a big talker, a natural leader. He was the first among the disciples to confess that Jesus was the Liberating King, and he

---

[12] Philippians 3:3.
[13] Yancey, *The Bible Jesus Read*, 55.
[14] Yancey, *Disappointment with God*, 201.
[15] Job 42:7–9.

was the one who dared to "correct" Jesus when Jesus predicted his death, "God forbid it, Lord. That shall never happen to you."[16] Jesus rebuked Peter, but Peter was undaunted. On the night that Jesus was betrayed by Judas, Jesus again told his friends about the suffering to come; Jesus predicted that his followers would be scattered. Peter spoke up, "Even if everyone else deserts you, I will never desert you . . . Even if I have to die with you, I will never deny you."[17] Not long after that declaration of P-Certainty, when Jesus was being tortured by the religious authorities, Peter's confidence disappeared. His P-Certainty was supplanted by doubt, and his doubt quickly morphed into fear. To protect himself in the mess of uncertainty, Peter denied Jesus: "A curse on me if I'm lying—I don't know the man!"[18] That was the end of Peter's P-Certainty. "He wept bitterly."[19] Jesus, after conquering death, restored and commissioned his friend.[20] The rest, of course, is history, as recorded in the Book of Acts and reflected in the Petrine epistles. Peter, the man of P-Certainty, became Peter, the man of H-Certainty. He was not delivered from the mess, but for the rest of his life—in the midst of the mess—"in various trials"— he learned to fix his "hope completely on grace" and to live by faith, "even though tested by fire."[21]

This brings us to the tension between faith and doubt. Is it possible for a person of faith to doubt? The answer is a qualified yes. It not only is possible, it is inevitable for people of faith

---

[16] Matthew 16:13–23.
[17] Matthew 26:31–35.
[18] Matthew 26:69–75.
[19] Matthew 26:75.
[20] John 21:15–17.
[21] 1 Peter 1:6–9.

to experience moments or even seasons of doubt. Consider, for example, David's desperate prayer in Psalm 13: "How long, YHWH? Will you forget me forever? How long will you hide your face from me?"[22] No one can question David's credentials as a man of faith. Yet, in a time of crisis—when David cried out to God, "Why have you forsaken me?"[23]—he was given no answer and no relief. At least that is how he felt.

Consider also John the Baptist. He was a true believer even before he was born. When Mary, with Jesus in her womb, entered the house of Elizabeth and greeted her, John "leaped for joy" in Elizabeth's womb.[24] Years later, when John returned from the wilderness to prepare the way for the Liberating King, he had no doubts that Jesus was the One. John's preaching—specifically his prophetic indictment of Herod and Herodias—resulted in his imprisonment,[25] but John was sure that the Liberating King would quickly "topple the mighty (including Herod) from their thrones, and exalt the lowly (including John)."[26] That did not happen, and John began to consider the possibility that he had been wrong about Jesus. John had doubt. John sent his disciples to ask Jesus a very blunt question: "Are you the Expected One, or should we expect someone else?"[27]

Finally, consider Mother Teresa. She was rightly regarded as a hero of faithfulness throughout her life. She served the poorest of the poor; she led an international ministry of compassion; she

---

[22] Psalm 13:1–2.
[23] Psalm 22:1–2.
[24] Luke 1:41.
[25] Matthew 6:17–18.
[26] Luke 1:52.
[27] Matthew 11:3.

spoke boldly and prophetically to the powerful on behalf of the powerless, including the unborn; and she was plagued by doubt. In private diaries and in letters to confessors, she wrote about her struggle. For example, in one diary entry, she wrote: "In my soul, I feel just the terrible pain of loss, of God not wanting me, of God not being God, of God not really existing."[28] This diary entry was not simply the result of one bad day. She struggled with profound and painful doubt for decades.

It is clear, therefore, that people of faith can and do doubt. Sometimes, God is hidden, and that is a "normal part of the pilgrimage of faith."[29] If you don't believe this, Phillip Yancey challenges you to "simply browse in a theological library among the works of the Christian mystics, men and women who have spent their lives in personal communion with God. Search for one, just one, who does not describe a time of severe testing, 'the dark night of the soul.'"[30]

So, if you struggle with doubt, you are in very good company. However, beware: just as there two types of certainty, there are two types of doubters. In their times of doubt, David, John the Baptist, and Mother Teresa asked God their hardest questions and expressed to God their darkest thoughts. They took to heart the bold message of the Book of Job: "You can say anything to God. Throw at him your grief, your anger, your doubt, your bitterness, your betrayal, your disappointment—he can absorb them."[31] They turned to God, and they kept turning to God, even in times

---

[28] Cindy Wooten, "Longing for God: Mother Teresa's letters reveal isolation, doubts," www.catholicnews.com.

[29] Yancey, *Disappointment with God*, 261.

[30] Ibid.

[31] Ibid., 263.

of extreme uncertainty, "when God stays silent, when nothing works according to the formula and all of the Bible's promises seem glaringly false."[32] They were humble doubters, "hanging on to the stubborn conviction that things are not as they appear,"[33] and that God will keep his promises, including the promises to be with them always and to make all things new. The defining characteristic of the humble doubter is the humble doubter's determination to believe in God and to know him. Brian McLaren is right, therefore, when he observes that doubt isn't a spiritual danger sign nearly as much as indifference would be.[34]

We live today in an age of proud doubters, professional skeptics, and celebrity atheists who write best-selling books to proselytize wavering theists and agnostics. These proud doubters, in their own way, are people of P-Certainty, even though some of them labor to deny it. Nica Lalli, for example, proudly identifies herself as an atheist, but insists that she has just enough uncertainty to avoid being arrogant:

> Let me be clear, I doubt the existence of god but I do not know that there is no god. I understand that there are non-believers out there who are certain of god's non-existence, but I prefer to stay in the Richard Dawkins camp on this one. He says that he is "almost certain that there is no god." This means that there is a sliver of doubt. And that tiny wedge of doubt keeps me from being arrogant. Because that tiny possibility means that I do not pretend to know it all. Knowing makes people too

---

[32] Ibid., 231–32.
[33] Ibid., 229.
[34] McLaren, *Finding Faith*, 203.

certain and that certainty makes people arrogant and ultimately insufferable—especially in a discussion about religion (or lack thereof).[35]

In this truly amazing quote, Lalli is commending herself for having just enough uncertainty ("a tiny wedge of doubt") to keep from being arrogant and insufferable. I guess I will have to take her word for that, but I suspect that she would not offer a comparable commendation of an outspoken theist who claimed to be "almost certain—with only a sliver of doubt—that the God of Abraham, Isaac, and Jacob is the one true God."

There is a lot that could be said about these proud doubters,[36] but I mention them in this essay only to make this point. Faith in Jesus is not compatible with proud certainty or proud doubt. Faith in Jesus requires humility in uncertainty and humility in doubt. There are many reasons to believe or disbelieve, but we will not persevere in faith unless we have the humility to "trust YHWH with all [our] heart . . . and not claim to be "wise in [our] own eyes."[37] In the midst of uncertainty and through seasons of doubt,

---

[35] Nica Lalli, "Mother Teresa's Doubts," www.huffingtonpost.com.

[36] One of the most formidable and celebrated proud doubters was the author Christopher Hitchens. His brother Peter has written a remarkable book about his own journey from atheism to faith, *The Rage Against God*. With humility and charity, he explains and deconstructs the motivations and arguments of the militant atheists. He contends that atheists are not dispassionate empiricists who are simply evaluating the evidence with rational, unsentimental objectivity. Rather, as Thomas Nagel, an atheist philosopher, admits, "I don't want there to be a God; I don't want the universe to be like that" (Hitchens, *The Rage Against God*, 150).

[37] Proverbs 3:5–6.

faith in Jesus humbly celebrates the certainty of God's faithfulness even though there is so much that we do not know:

> Only at the end of time, after we have obtained God's level of viewing, after every evil has been punished or forgiven, every illness healed and the universe restored . . . only then will fairness reign. Then we will understand what role is played by evil, and by the Fall, and by natural law in an unfair event like the death of a child. Until then, we will not know, and can only trust God who does know. We remain ignorant of many details, not because God enjoys keeping us in the dark, but because we have not the faculties to absorb so much light . . . Not until history has run its course will we understand how "all things work together for good." Faith means believing in advance what will only make sense in reverse.[38]

God, protect us from proud certainty and proud doubt. Lord, we believe. Help us in our unbelief. Amen.

---

[38] Yancey, *Disappointment with God*, 224.

CHAPTER 9

UNITY

In June of 1972, I was into a lot of things, but I was not into Christianity. One hot summer day, I turned on the family television and scanned our six channels, without the benefit of a remote control. Life was hard in those days. I stopped changing channels when I saw two of my musical heroes, Johnny Cash and Kris Kristofferson, singing to 100,000 suspicious looking young people somewhere in Dallas. I had stumbled onto Explo '72, the so-called Christian Woodstock. I watched the show, and tried to figure out what my heroes were doing with that bunch of fanatical faux hippies. I don't remember many details. In fact, I only remember one detail. At some point, I think it may have been the grand finale, the whole bunch of them were singing a catchy little tune, "We are one in the Spirit / We are one in the Lord / and we pray that all unity / will someday be restored." I have to admit that—in spite of my effort to remain detached—I was touched by the sight and sound of all of those people singing that song together. I had to consider the possibility that they might be onto something. I actually wanted to find out more about these Jesus people and their faith.

In John 17, Jesus prayed for his disciples, and for all of those who would shift their allegiance to him through their message. That prayer, therefore, is for all of us, and it shows the heart of Jesus:

> May they all be one, just as you, Father, are in me and I am in you. May they also be one in us, so that the world may believe you sent me. I have given them the glory that you have given to me. May they be one just as we are one. I am in them and you are in me. May they may be made completely one, so that all people in the world may know you sent me and that you have loved them just as you have loved me.[1]

Jesus prayed for unity, oneness, so that the people who are trapped in the bogus world system will know that the Father sent Jesus to show his love. That always has been God's plan, to call out a people who will be his witnesses to his grace:

> At Pentecost God created a new language, but it was a language that was more than words. It is instead a community whose memory of its Savior creates the miracle of being a people whose very differences contribute to their unity. We call this new creation church. It is constituted by word and sacrament, as the story we tell, the story we embody, must not only be told but enacted. In the telling we are challenged to be a people capable of hearing God's good news such that we can be a witness to

---

[1] John 17:21–23.

others. In the enactment, in baptism and Eucharist, we are made part of a common history that requires continual celebration to be rightly remembered. It is through baptism and Eucharist that our lives are engrafted onto the life of the One that makes our unity possible.[2]

That plan, sadly, has been compromised by a lack of unity among God's people. This lack of unity contradicts the message of Jesus and sabotages evangelism. If Jesus' followers do not love one another, it is much easier to dismiss or disregard the gospel.

The problem started at the earliest stage of church history, and it even infected relatively healthy first-century churches such as the church at Philippi. This is one of the reasons Paul wrote Philippians. A little bit of background information will shed some light on this letter. Philippi was a Roman colony, and the proud citizens of that city considered that status to be a very big deal.[3] Patriotic and responsible Roman citizens were expected to confess that Caesar was lord and savior.[4] Jesus' people could not do that; their refusal to participate in that patriotic practice created tension and external opposition.[5] Paul was familiar with this type of tension and opposition. He actually was in a Roman jail when he wrote the letter. Apparently, the external opposition was creating internal conflict and disunity among Jesus' people in Philippi. Paul saw this as a serious threat to the mission.

Paul tackles this problem in the section that starts with Philippians 1:27. He exhorts them to do their duty as citizens—not

---

[2] Hauerwas, *The Hauerwas Reader*, 149.
[3] Fee, *Paul's Letter to the Philippians*, 25.
[4] Ibid., 31.
[5] Ibid., 31–33.

of Rome, but of God's kingdom.⁶ This duty entails practical unity and concerted action: "Standing firm in one Spirit, with one mind, struggling side by side for the faith of the gospel."⁷ A few verses later, Paul reiterates and expands that exhortation with a personal plea: "Make my joy complete by thinking the same way, having the same love, sharing the same feelings, focusing on the same goal."⁸

How are the Philippians supposed to achieve and maintain that unity? Two simple steps: 1) don't act out of selfish ambition or empty conceit to protect your own interests, instead 2) in humility, consider others more important than yourself, and focus on protecting their interests.⁹ Okay, those steps are not simple. In fact, without God, they are impossible. Paul's point, though, is that unity is necessary for the mission of the gospel, and humility is necessary for unity.

The most compelling role model for humility is Jesus:

> Make your attitude that of Jesus the Liberating
>   King,
> Who, existing in the form of God,
> did not consider equality with God
> as something to be used for his own advantage.
> Instead he emptied himself
> by assuming the form of a slave,
> taking on the likeness of man.

---

[6] Ibid. 161, n. 21 (discussing the imperative *politeuesthe*); see also Philippians 1:27 in Today's New International Version (TNIV).

[7] Philippians 1:27.

[8] Philippians 2:2.

[9] Philippians 2:3–4.

> And when he had come as a man,
> he humbled himself
> by becoming obedient to the point of death—
> even death on a cross.[10]

This is the normative pattern for citizens of God's kingdom. Our corporate life—our story—must take the shape of Jesus' story of obedient self-emptying and self-giving love on the cross.[11] Michael Gorman uses the term "cruciformity" (from cruciform, meaning cross-shaped) to refer to "this conformity to the crucified Christ."[12] The way to unity is through cruciform community.

Paul provides additional insight into the nexus between humility and unity in Ephesians:

> I, therefore, as a prisoner in the Lord, urge you to walk worthy of the calling you have received, with all humility and gentleness, with patience, accepting one another in love, diligently keeping the unity of the Spirit with the peace that binds us. There is one body and one Spirit, just as you were called to one hope at your calling; one Lord, one faith, one baptism, one God and Father of all, who is above all and to all and in all.[13]

Gordon Fee observes that the goal of the exhortation to "walk worthy" is the maintenance of the "unity of the Spirit in the bond

---

[10] Philippians 2:5–8.

[11] Gorman, *Cruciformity*, 350 (discussing the "corporate character of cruciformity"; "To be in Christ is to live within a community that is shaped by his story").

[12] Gorman, *Apostle of the Crucified Lord*, 140.

[13] Ephesians 4:1–6.

of shalom."[14] That goal is only achievable through the virtues of humility, gentleness, patience, and love. The point, according to Fee, is that the unity that binds Jesus' people "by virtue of their common experience of the Spirit will be maintained only as the Spirit produces the virtues necessary for it."[15]

Almost two thousand years after Jesus prayed for unity, and Paul exhorted churches to unity, Jesus' people appear to be permanently and irrevocably divided by denominations, theologies, ethnicities, ideologies, and styles. But there are hopeful signs. Young Life, Living Water, Compassion International, and other cooperative missional endeavors bring folks together for Kingdom work. When we pull together for mission, the Holy Spirit reminds us that our common identity in Christ trumps our differences and distinctives.

One of my seminary professors, Richard Lovelace, advocated this type of "unitive evangelicalism."[16] My congregation is not perfect. Actually, my congregation is not even close to perfect, but we have taken a cue from Dr. Lovelace. When we composed our statement of faith, we intentionally sought out "the minimal circle of biblical truth which guarantees the honor of God and the spiritual health of believers" so that we could "make the biblical church approximate the invisible as closely as possible."[17] Our rationale is simple. We do not want to be a church that would—on doctrinal grounds—exclude John the Baptist, John Chrysostom, John Calvin, John Wesley, John Owen, John Stott, John Howard

---

[14] Fee, *God's Empowering Presence*, 699–701.

[15] Ibid.

[16] Lovelace, *Dynamics of Spiritual Life*, 312 (contrasting separatist and inclusivist ecclesiologies).

[17] Ibid.

Yoder, Joni Eareckson Tada, or Johnny Cash, although I seriously doubt that any of these amazing Christian folks (except possibly Johnny Cash) would put up with a rag-tag group of knuckleheads like us.

Of course, a unitive statement of faith—by itself—does not produce unity. That is the work of the Spirit who produces the essential virtues—starting with humility—that make unity a reality. John Stott's prescription for a "fresh unity" among Jesus' people emphasizes the Spirit's role and the need for humility:

> We must come to the biblical text with a recognition of our cultural prejudices and with the willingness to have them challenged and changed. If we come to Scripture with the proud presupposition that all of our inherited beliefs and practices are correct, then of course we shall find in the Bible only what we want to find, namely the comfortable confirmation of the status quo. As a result, we shall also find ourselves in sharp disagreement with people who come to Scripture from different backgrounds and different convictions and find these confirmed. There is probably no commoner source of discord than this. It is only when we are brave and humble enough to allow the Spirit of God through the Word of God radically to call in question our most cherished opinions, that we are likely to find fresh unity through fresh understanding.[18]

Jesus prayed for unity. As our high priest and advocate, he is still praying.

---

[18] Stott, *God's Book for God's People*, 50.

Lord, we thank you for showing us the way of cruciform community. Forgive us for our selfish ambition and empty conceit, and the disunity that we cause, often out of pride. Holy Spirit, produce humility, gentleness, patience, and love in and among us so we can be one. Amen.

CHAPTER 10

REALITY

Stanley Hauerwas has argued that "the failure to live with humility, a failure common to Christian and non-Christian alike, results in a distorted understanding of the way things are."[1] I agree with that, of course, but I think the converse is equally true: a distorted understanding of the way things are results in a lack of humility. My theory is that we will get humility if we grasp reality.

A potential objection to my theory is that the very idea or concept of "reality" is controversial. The word itself has been debased and devalued. Take, for example, "reality television." Most of us have figured out that reality television presents carefully orchestrated and highly contrived narratives for commercial and entertainment purposes. Reality television is show business, and it is only slightly more "real" than *The Simpsons*.

In addition to the denotative problem, there is the epistemological problem. Some very educated people, for a variety of

---

[1] Hauerwas, *Performing the Faith*, 127.

philosophical, sociolinguistic, and personal reasons, categorically reject any claims concerning unitary, definitive, or absolute reality. In *Exploring Reality*, scientist-theologian John Polkinghorne, discusses this development:

> "Reality," and the closely-allied word "truth," are not in common currency in some circles today, and consequently those who employ them lay themselves open to intellectual condescension and pity . . . The extreme wing of the movement loosely categorized as postmodernism has suggested that instead of truth about reality, we have to settle for a portfolio of opinions expressing personal or societal points of view. Though there may appear to be conflicts between the different perspectives proposed, it is said that there is no real competition between them because, in fact, there is not actually anything to contend about. All points of view can claim equal authenticity, since none is constrained by an independently accessible external reality.[2]

I am not qualified to address the debates about modernity and post-modernity, but I have noticed how the dismissal of any "independently accessible external reality" is impacting everyday life in the bubba-burbs, where I live and love and eat barbecue.

Specifically, it has become fashionable—if not yet normative—for people to think, speak, and act in terms of multiple or alternative subjectively determined realities. "You have your reality, and I have mine." In the realm of religion, this approach may emphasize the need to "be at peace with God, whatever you conceive him

---

[2] Polkinghorne, *Exploring Reality*, 1–2.

to be."[3] This approach has some superficial appeal. For example, it seems to avoid the arrogance that comes with being a theological know-it-all. Upon closer examination, however, it is pretty arrogant to make yourself the arbiter of reality, and it is vacuous diffidence to delegate the task to another person or group of people.

The real problem with this "be-at-peace-with-God-whatever-you-or-I-conceive-him-to-be" approach is that God—if he does exist—is who he is, no matter what we may or may not conceive him to be. And further, if God does exist, he is the arbiter of reality, the *ens realissimum* (the most real being), and the ultimate issue is whether or how God is knowable. If God exists, and is knowable, then reality is not relative; rather, reality is relational, personal.[4]

The same may be said about truth. Thomas Aquinas's classic definition of truth "designates truth as '*adaequatio intellectus et rei*' (conformity between the intellect and reality)."[5] If we accurately perceive "a thing as it is in itself," then we have found truth,

---

[3] This is a line from one of the worst recordings of the 1970s, "Desiderata." The National Lampoon recorded a brilliant parody of "Desiderata," called "Deteriorata." In "Deteriorata," the listener is urged to "be at peace with God whatever you conceive him to be, be he Hairy Thunderer or Cosmic Muffin." This great line succinctly articulates two common misconceptions about God.

[4] Polkinghorne argues that Divine Reality is relational because of God's Trinity: "Divine intrinsic relationality is totally fulfilled in the perichoretic exchanges between the Persons, and so God's creative action is not demanded by any impulse to meet a divine need for the external supplementation of that relationship. Nevertheless, the relational nature of deity is perfectly expressed … [by] the generous act of bringing into being a world which is the object of divine love" (Polkinghorne, *Exploring Reality*, 112).

[5] Ratzinger, *Jesus of Nazareth: From the Entrance into Jerusalem to the Resurrection*, 192.

"a fragment of reality."[6] But if God exists, and is knowable, then this classic definition of truth, although useful, is not adequate. Aquinas recognized this when he wrote that God is "*ipsa summa et prima veritas*" (truth itself, the sovereign and first truth).[7] Ultimately, truth is relational and personal, a *who* not a *what*. To know God is to know Truth.

The God we encounter in Scripture is "not tame."[8] Consider, for example, Isaiah's vision of YHWH and his heavenly council.

> In the year of King Uzziah's death, I saw the Lord seated on a high, elevated throne. The hem of his robe filled the temple. Seraphs stood over him; each one had six wings. With two wings they covered their faces, with two they covered their feet, and they used the other two to fly. They called out to one another:
> "Holy, holy, holy is YHWH of Hosts:
> His glory fills the whole earth."
> The foundation of the doorways shook at the sound of their voices, and the temple was filled with smoke.[9]

In light of the vision, Isaiah knew exactly where he stood:

> Woe is me, for I am ruined,
> Because I am a man of unclean lips
> And live among a people of unclean lips.
> [And] because I have seen the King,

---

[6] Ibid.

[7] Ibid.

[8] This phrase is borrowed from C. S. Lewis's description of Aslan, the Christ-figure, in *The Chronicles of Narnia*.

[9] Isaiah 6:1–4.

YHWH of Hosts.[10]

Also consider John's vision of Jesus, the "firstborn from the dead, the King of kings":

> He was dressed in a robe extending down to his feet and he wore a wide golden belt around his chest. His head and hair were as white as wool, even as white as snow, and his eyes were like a fiery flame. His feet were like polished bronze refined in a furnace, and his voice was like the roar of many waters. He held seven stars in his right hand, and a sharp double-edged sword extended out of his mouth. His face shone like the sun shining at full strength.[11]

John was terrified: "When I saw him I fell down at his feet as though I were dead."[12]

The God of Scripture is truly awesome in the fullest and deepest sense of that word. He speaks out of the whirlwind, with incomparable glory and power.[13] He is a "consuming fire,"[14] and his "greatness is unsearchable."[15] God is "wholly other."[16] But he is knowable because he has revealed himself definitively in Jesus;

---

[10] Isaiah 6:5.

[11] Revelation 1:13–16.

[12] Revelation 1:17. This awe-struck response echoes Ezekiel's response to the glory of YHWH in Ezekiel 1:21: "When I saw [the glory], I fell on my face."

[13] Job 38:1.

[14] Hebrews 12:29.

[15] Psalm 145:3.

[16] Barth, *The Humanity of God*, 37.

the Eternal Word humbled himself to become the Incarnate Word, "full of grace and truth."[17]

This, of course, is the goal of the gospel, that we "may know the one true God and Jesus the Liberating King."[18] This is not an intellectual exercise, even though it involves the mind along with the heart. We may deduce or induce that God exists, but knowing him is a supernatural and supra-rational blessing. Knowing God is a gracious work of the Holy Spirit, so anyone who knows God should know that he or she has no bragging rights. We know God only by the grace of God. Karl Barth makes this point well:

> For the sake of the veracity of our knowledge of God, the veracity of the revelation of God will necessarily make us humble. By the grace of God we shall truly know God with our views and concepts, and truly speak of God with our words. But we shall not be able to boast about it, as if it is our own success, and we have performed and done it.[19]

In the first three chapters of Ephesians, Paul writes about the blessings that God has lavished on those who are "in Christ," which is shorthand for those who by grace through faith "have been rescued from the dominion of darkness and transferred into the kingdom of his beloved Son."[20] Paul prays twice for his readers to know God as he really is.

In the first prayer, Paul asks God to give them the "Spirit of wisdom and revelation" so they can "know him better" and

---

[17] John 1:14.
[18] John 17:3.
[19] Barth, *Church Dogmatics*, 213.
[20] Colossians 1:13.

specifically that the "eyes of [their] heart may be enlightened" so that they may know his "incomparably great power" which is for his people.[21] In the second prayer, Paul prays that the Spirit will strengthen them "with power" so Jesus "may dwell in their hearts through faith" and they will grasp the immeasurable "breadth, length, height, and depth" of Jesus' love, and will personally experience "this love that surpasses knowledge."[22] These two prayers, taken together, are for God's people to personally know God and experience his incomparable power and immeasurable love.

This is how and what we ought to pray for ourselves and for others: that the Holy Spirit will give us a daily reality check, that we will regularly and deliberately discard our reoccurring misconceptions about God and really know him, experiencing his all-surpassing power and his mind-boggling love. If we grasp Divine Reality—if we know God as he is—we will get humility.

> Humility rests upon a Holy blindness, like the blindness of him who looks steadily into the sun. For wherever he turns his eyes on earth, there he sees only the sun. The God-blinded soul sees naught of self, naught of personal degradation or of personal eminence, but only the Holy Will.[23]

Søren Kierkegaard, based on his understanding of the "absolute difference between God and man," found solace in "the humility that frankly admits its human lowliness with humble cheerfulness before God, trusting that God knows all this better than

---

[21] Ephesians 1:15–21.
[22] Ephesians 3:14–19.
[23] Kelly, *A Testament of Devotion*, 69.

man himself."[24] This point is made clear in the opening verses to Ephesians 4. After Paul prays that his friends will know God as he really is, Paul urges them to live out the reality of knowing God by walking with "complete humility and gentleness,"[25] imitating the Truth who humbled himself by becoming obedient to the point of death, even death on a cross.[26]

With this daily reality check, we can avoid the mistake of "thinking too highly"[27] of ourselves, without falling into the trap of forgetting who we are by God's grace.

God, we pray that your Spirit will give us the power to know you better, and we pray that knowing your power and love will enable us to walk with complete humility and gentleness. Amen.

---

[24] Kierkegaard, "Postscript to the Philosophical Fragments," 246.
[25] Ephesians 4:1–2.
[26] Philippians 2:8.
[27] Romans 12:3.

CHAPTER 11

LIBERTY

The gospel is the prototypical freedom song.[1] "For liberty the Liberating King has liberated us."[2] In the context of Galatians, this emancipation proclamation makes it clear that Jesus sets people free from the hostile powers[3] of sin and death, and also from the custody of the law.[4] However, that proclamation is only the first verse of the freedom song. The freedom song is not simply about what Jesus sets us free *from*, but also what Jesus sets us free *for*.

---

[1] In American history, the first freedom songs were sung by slaves. These seemingly innocent "spirituals" with themes of hope and endurance were deeply subversive on multiple levels. The songs often included coded messages. For example, "This Train is Bound for Glory" had an intentional double reference to heaven and to the Underground Railroad. See Owen Sound's Black history, at www.osblackhistory.com.

[2] Galatians 5:1.

[3] Galatians 4:3.

[4] Galatians 3:24–25.

It is a spiritual fact that we cannot handle freedom, apart from the power of the Holy Spirit. On the one hand, some of us are tempted by a legalistic impulse to return to the perceived security and stability of religious codes and regulations. Paul emphatically warns us not to "submit again to a yoke of slavery,"[5] but we do it anyway. Paul chastises us for this absurd choice: "Why do you submit to regulations: 'Don't handle, don't taste, don't touch'?"[6] There are many possible explanations for this puzzling phenomenon, including our tendency to take pride in our compliance with certain rules, but there are no viable or acceptable explanations. Simply stated, Jesus did not break us out of prison so we could *return* to prison.

On the other hand, some of us are tempted by a libertarian impulse. Paul addresses this impulse with equally emphatic language:

> For you are called to liberty, brothers and sisters; do not use this liberty as an opportunity for selfish or rebellious inclinations, but perform the duties of a slave for one another through love. For the entire law is fulfilled in one statement: You shall love your neighbor as yourself. For if you bite and devour one another, watch out, or you will be consumed by one another.[7]

In his response to the libertarian impulse, Paul describes the purpose of freedom in negative and positive terms. First, Jesus does not set us free for the purpose of selfishness, so that we can do whatever we want to do, whenever we want to do it. This abuse

---

[5] Galatians 5:2.
[6] Colossians 2:20–21.
[7] Galatians 5:13–15.

of freedom, based on a crass misunderstanding of grace, has been and continues to be a disaster for the church. The root cause is pride, more particularly a refusal to surrender our proud delusions of individual sovereignty and walk in humility by the power of the Holy Spirit. Gordon Fee explains this point as follows:

> "Freedom" has nothing to do with selfishness, meaning freedom to do whatever one wants, whenever one wants to. Using a word having to do with a "base of operations" for further activity, Paul indicates what "freedom in Christ" does not mean; it is not to serve as a "base of operations" for "the flesh." The word "flesh," which first appeared in [Galatians] 3:13 in this letter, will finally be defined—in terms of its actions—in vv. 19–21, selfish actions all.[8]

In positive terms, Jesus sets us free so we can *voluntarily* "perform the duties of a slave for one another through love."[9] This paradox is predicated on the example of the One who existed "in the form of God," but who—rather than using his status for his own advantage—humbled himself, assuming "the form of a slave" and being executed on a Roman cross as a demonstration of divine love.[10] In sum, we are set free from pride and for humility.

In our culture, we tend to confuse and conflate two different types of freedom. As citizens of the United States, heirs to and beneficiaries of the American political tradition, and particularly the Bill of Rights, we have the freedom to speak, worship, and

---

[8] Fee, *Galatians*, 203–4.
[9] This is a literal translation of the verb *douleuete*. See ibid., 204.
[10] Philippians 2:6–8; Romans 5:8.

assemble without government coercion or interference. These fundamental freedoms are framed and defended as civil rights. Fighting for and asserting one's civil rights are quintessentially American activities. In a sense, as Americans, we tend to define ourselves in terms of our rights.

As citizens of the kingdom of God, we have been set free from bondage to the hostile powers of sin and death, and we have been given the amazing "right to be children of God."[11] Our focus, however, "as dearly loved children," should not be on asserting any of our purported rights, but on our duty to "be imitators of God" by "walk[ing] in love as the Liberating King [who] loved us and gave himself for us."[12] As followers of Jesus, we should not define ourselves in terms of our rights under any political theory or system, but in terms of our duty to love by the power of the Spirit.

In his critique of the liberation theology of Gustavo Gutierrez, Stanley Hauerwas makes this same point:

> For the salvation promised in the good news is not a life free from suffering, free from servitude, but rather a life that freely serves, that freely suffers, because such suffering and service is the hallmark of the Kingdom established by Jesus. As Christians, we do not seek to be free but rather to be of use, for it is only by serving that we discover the freedom offered by God.[13]

---

[11] John 1:12; Galatians 4:6.
[12] Ephesians 5:1–2.
[13] Hauerwas, *After Christendom?*, 53–54.

That certainly does not mean that we are or should be indifferent to or complacent about the relative advantages of political and economic freedom, limited government, and the constitutional system of checks and balances. We can and should be thankful for our rights and liberties as Americans, and it is entirely proper for us—as an expression of love—to participate in a peaceful struggle to vindicate the rights and liberties of those who cannot speak for themselves. But we cross the line when we put the emphasis on our own rights. "True freedom is not freedom from responsibility to God and others in order to live for ourselves, but freedom from ourselves in order to live for God and others."[14] "Freedom literally comes by having our self-absorption challenged by the needs of another."[15]

The gospel, therefore, sets us free *from* pride and *for* service to the King who humbled himself for us. To truly live free, we must get low.

The freedom song of the Kingdom is about duty, not rights. Our freedom is secured, defined, and shaped by the cross. Lord, we thank you for setting us free from the tyranny of sin and death. By the power of your Holy Spirit, may we imitate the humility of Jesus as slaves of cruciform love. Amen.

---

[14] Stott, *The Gospel and the End of Time*, 91.
[15] Hauerwas, *After Christendom?*, 54.

CHAPTER 12

FAMILY

As a general rule, the lexicon of country music lyrics may not be the best place to seek marital advice. However, I have heard few sermons and read few books that can match the insights of George Jones and Roger Miller. If you can listen to George Jones sing "He Stopped Loving Her Today" without crying and/or re-committing to your spouse, then you, my friend, are a heartless cyborg. Jones (a.k.a. the Possum) learned every life lesson the hard way. One of those lessons is imbedded in "The Race is On," which uses a horse race as a metaphor for a break-up. The first lines of the chorus are "now the race is on, and here comes pride up the backstretch, heartache coming to the inside..." The punch line of the chorus is deceptively profound: "and the winner loses all."[1] The Possum's point is well-taken: pride destroys relationships. Roger Miller makes the same point in his song "Husbands and Wives":

---

[1] George Jones, "The Race is On," *The Race is On* (United Artists, 1964).

Family

> It's my belief
> pride is the chief cause
> of the decline
> in the number
> of husbands and wives.[2]

I suspect that the Apostle Paul would have loved real country music. After all, in spite of his impressive professional credentials (as a Pharisee trained by Gamaliel), he was a blue-collar guy (a tentmaker) who rambled from town to town and often got thrown into jail. That is the stuff of real country music. Among New Testament scholars, Paul's affinity for real country music may be an open question. There is no question, however, that Paul, George Jones, and Roger Miller are on the same page when it comes to the destructive impact of the lack of humility on familial relationships.

Paul's most comprehensive (and most controversial) teaching on marriage and family is in Ephesians 5:22—6:4. This passage, of course, must be understood in context. The first three chapters of the letter are in the indicative mood. In those chapters, Paul describes what it means to be "seated in the heavens, in the realm of Jesus the Liberating King."[3] Paul prays that we might know God intimately, experiencing his incomparable power and immeasurable love.[4]

---

[2] Roger Miller, "Husbands and Wives," *Words and Music* (Smash Records, 1966).

[3] Ephesians 2:6.

[4] Ephesians 1:15-19; 3:14-19.

Chapters 4 through 6 are in the imperative mood. Paul exhorts us to live out the reality described in the first three chapters. The controlling imperative from Ephesians 4:1—6:9 is to "walk in a manner worthy of the calling [we] have received with all humility and gentleness."[5] Among other things, this entails "forgiving one another, just as God also forgave [us],"[6] and imitating God in cruciform love.[7] Mutual forgiveness and cruciform love require humility. Everything that Paul says about marital and familial relationships is contingent on fidelity to these basic precepts.

The immediate context for Paul's teaching on marriage and family begins in Ephesians 5:18. Paul commands us not to "get drunk with wine, which leads to waste," but, instead, to be "continually filled with the Spirit." How does one get filled with the Spirit? The answer to this question may be found in John 7, where Jesus invites those who are thirsty to come to him and drink, and promises that the ones who thirst and drink will be filled with streams or torrents of living water.[8] This is a reference to the power of the Holy Spirit. The key to fullness, therefore, is being humble enough 1) to admit a need (thirst), 2) to go to Jesus, and 3) to surrender with radical trust.

In Ephesians 5:19-21, Paul uses four participial phrases to describe the evidence or effects of being filled with the Spirit: 1) "speaking to one another in psalms, hymns, and spiritual songs"; 2) "singing and making music to the Lord"; 3) "giving thanks

---

[5] Ephesians 4:1-2.
[6] Ephesians 4:32.
[7] Ephesians 5:1-2.
[8] John 7:37-39.

always for everything"; and 4) "submitting to one another in fear of the Liberating King."[9]

The last effect—mutual submission—sets the table for Paul's words to husbands and wives, and parents and children. In fact, in the Greek text, Ephesians 5:22 does not even have a verb. The lack of a verb signals grammatical and logical dependence on the preceding verses.[10] Translators properly borrow the verb "submit" from the participial phrase in Ephesians 5:21, which of course depends on the command to be continually filled with the Spirit, which requires humility.

With that context in mind, by the power of the Spirit, wives are called to "submit to [their] husbands as to the Lord."[11] There is nothing coercive in this text. Submission is a voluntary act that can be performed only by free and responsible persons. Peter O'Brien explains the meaning and significance of this voluntary act:

> The keyword rendered "submit" has to do with the subordination of someone in an ordered array to another who is above the first, that is, in authority over that person. At the heart of this submission is the notion of "order." God has established certain leadership and authority roles within the family, and submission is a humble recognition of that divine ordering.[12]

This call to subordination in marriage has been misconstrued and abused. In some families and faith communities, the call to subordination by the wife has been used as a pretext for tyranny

---

[9] Ephesians 5:19–21.
[10] O'Brien, *The Letter to the Ephesians*, 411.
[11] Ephesians 5:22.
[12] O'Brien, *The Letter to the Ephesians*, 411.

by the husband. This is a demonic distortion of biblical submission. Some have twisted this passage to suggest that women are inferior to men, or, at least, that Paul regarded women as inferior to men. This suggestion ignores Jesus' submission to the Father, which shows us that voluntary submission denotes a "functional subordination without implying inferiority, or less glory and honor."[13] The call to submit is Christ-centered; the submission must be "as to the Lord," for Jesus' sake and in response to his cruciform love. This type of humility is impossible without the Holy Spirit.

By the power of the Spirit, husbands have the correlative duty to "love their wives just as the Liberating King loved the church and gave himself up for her."[14] This is not a hyperbole. Husbands are called to imitate the One who—as the ultimate expression of love—"humbled himself and became obedient to the point of death, even death on a cross."[15] That means, among other things, that a husband must put his wife's interests ahead of his own interests in matters great and small. This type of humility is impossible without the Holy Spirit.

By the power of the Spirit, children are called to "obey [their] parents in the Lord, for this is right."[16] This call assumes that children are full participants in the life of the church. Paul addresses them as moral agents who are accountable for their actions, and who are held to a standard ("this is right") as followers of Jesus ("in the Lord"). Their duty to obey is not "simply because of their

---

[13] Ibid.
[14] Ephesians 5:25.
[15] Philippians 2:8.
[16] Ephesians 6:1.

parents' greater authority or status" in the culture or the church.[17] Their duty to obey is an essential expression of their discipleship. Sons and daughters are called to follow the Son who humbly prayed to the Father, "not my will but yours be done."[18] This type of humility is impossible without the Holy Spirit.

By the power of the Spirit, fathers have the duty to not "provoke their children to anger; instead to nourish them in the training and instruction of the Lord."[19] Under the Roman doctrine of *patria potestas*, the father had unlimited power over his children.[20] Paul makes it clear that this doctrine does not apply among followers of Jesus. Effectively, Paul is prohibiting "excessively severe discipline, unreasonably harsh demands, abuse of authority, arbitrariness, unfairness, constant nagging and condemnation, subjecting a child to humiliation, and all forms of gross insensitivity to a child's needs and sensibilities."[21] Paul exhorts fathers to nourish their children through Christ-centered training and instruction.[22] Paul's concern is not simply that the children be given correct information about Jesus, but that children experience the reality of God's love in and through their earthly fathers. With that in mind, fathers must humbly recognize that they cannot do what God has called them to do by their own authority and power. This type of humility is impossible without the Holy Spirit.

---

[17] O'Brien, *The Letter to the Ephesians*, 441.
[18] Luke 22:42.
[19] Ephesians 6:4.
[20] O'Brien, *The Letter to the Ephesians*, 445.
[21] Ibid., 446.
[22] Ephesians 6:4.

We cannot be the wives, husbands, children, and parents we are called to be without a healthy does of humility and, through the power of the Spirit, putting aside our pride.

―•―

Father, forgive us for our pride, and fill us with the power to imitate the humility of Jesus in all of our relationships, and particularly in our families. Amen.

CHAPTER 13

IDEOLOGY

Jesus was not apolitical, but he displayed negligible interest and no confidence in the politics of the bogus world system. He rejected the political ideologies and strategies of his day, including the pragmatic conservatism of the Herodians and Sadducees, the passive-aggressive pietism of the Pharisees, the communitarian isolationism of the Essenes, and the liberation theology of the Zealots.[1] He resisted the tempter's offer of "the kingdoms of the bogus world system and all their glory."[2] He evaded the mob that wanted to make him a king "by force."[3] He expressed casual indifference to Caesar and his coins.[4] He expressed clear contempt towards the arrogance of Herod Antipas.[5] He never attempted

---

[1] Yoder, *The Original Revolution*, 18–27.
[2] Matthew 4:8–10.
[3] John 6:15.
[4] Mark 12:17.
[5] Luke 13:32.

to forge any alliances with the high and mighty or the rich and famous, and he generally avoided the centers of political power. He spent most of his time in nowhere towns hanging out with so-called nobodies.

Jesus was not apolitical. He preached the gospel of the kingdom of God. He called people to change their way of thinking, to shift their allegiance away from the world's system to God's kingdom.[6] He made it clear that citizens of his kingdom are called to a distinctive social ethic, a Kingdom ethic, based on God's character, exemplified by his love for enemies.[7] In spite of his teaching, some of his best friends misconstrued his message and his mission. They thought he was going to take charge, Maccabean-style,[8] and they were vying for positions of power and status in the new regime. Jesus responded:

> The authority figures of the nations play this game, flexing their muscles in competition for power over one another, masking their quest for domination behind words like "benefactor" or "public servant." But you must not indulge in this charade.

---

[6] Mark 1:15.

[7] The Sermon on the Mount serves as the manifesto of God's kingdom. The heart of the manifesto is the call in Matthew 5:49 to "be *teleioi* as your Heavenly Father is *telos*." In context, it is clear that this is not a call to replicate God's metaphysical and moral perfection, but to imitate his love for enemies. Cf. Romans 5:10; see also Yoder, *The Original Revolution*, 47 ("We are asked to 'resemble God' at just this one point: not in His omnipotence or His eternity or His impeccability, but simply in the undiscriminating or unconditional character of his love.").

[8] "The Maccabean," which probably means "the hammer-like one," was the surname given to Judas, a Jewish hero who led and inspired a Jewish revolt against Syrian occupation of Palestine (Lohse, *New Testament Environment*, 126–27). Judas the Maccabean was killed in 160 B.C.

Instead, among you, the greatest must become like the youngest and the leader must become a true servant. Who is greater right here as we eat this meal—those of us who sit at the table, or those who serve us? Doesn't everyone normally assume those who are served are greater than those who serve? But consider My role among you. I have been with you as a servant.[9]

Jesus was not apolitical, but his kingdom is predicated on a radically and qualitatively different type of political action. The kingdoms of our bogus world system are established and maintained by a combination of coercive power and duplicitous beneficence. The kings of those kingdoms are prone to the sin of pride.[10]

The kingdom of God is established and maintained by humility and service. Jesus is the paradigm: the King who lays aside his robe, puts on the towel of humility, and washes feet.[11] The contrast between God's kingdom and the kingdoms of the bogus world system was reiterated and amplified when Pilate questioned Jesus about the allegation that Jesus was "king of the Jews":

> "My kingdom is not part of this bogus world system," said Jesus. "If my kingdom were part of this bogus world system, my servants would fight, so that I wouldn't be handed over to those

---

[9] Luke 22:25-27 (*The Voice*, with one modification: I translate *ethnoi* as "nations" rather than "outsiders").

[10] The Hebrew Scriptures make it clear that pride and arrogance are occupational hazards for kings and other political figures. Examples include Uzziah (2 Chronicles 26:15), Hezekiah (2 Chronicles 32:25), Nebuchadnezzar (Daniel 4:30), Belshazzar (Daniel 5:22-23), and the infamous King of Tyre (Ezekiel 28:2-19).

[11] John 13:4-5.

who are clamoring for my execution. As it is, my kingdom does not have its origins here."[12]

The kingdoms of the bogus world system are secured and defended by violence. Jesus' kingdom is radically different. It is secured by suffering love. Jesus fought and won the decisive battle for his kingdom by humbling himself and dying on a Roman cross. "The cross is the scepter and the sword of this Kingdom."[13] Jesus' followers are called to imitate him in humility and cruciform love. This is the way of the Kingdom.

> By God's design, this is how the kingdom of God expands and transforms the world. As we allow Christ's character to be formed in us—as we think and act like Jesus—others come under the loving influence of the kingdom and eventually their own hearts are won over to the King of kings. The reign of God is thus established in their hearts, and the kingdom of God expands. That process, Scripture tells us, will culminate in the return of the King accompanied by legions of angels, at which time Satan's rule will end, the earth will be purged of all that is inconsistent with God's rule, and his kingdom of love will be established once and for all.
>
> This, in a nutshell, is the primary thing God is up to in our world. He's not primarily about getting people to pray a magical "sinner's prayer" or to confess certain magical truths as a means of escaping hell. He's not about gathering together a group who happen to believe all the right things. Rather, he's about gathering together a group of people who embody

---

[12] John 18:36.

[13] Ward, *Politics of Discipleship*, 291.

the kingdom—who individually and corporately manifest the reality of the reign of God on the earth. And he's about growing this new kingdom through his body to take over the world. The vision of what God is about lies at the heart of Jesus's ministry, and it couldn't contrast with the kingdom of the world more sharply.[14]

How do Jesus people—the citizens of God's kingdom—relate to the kingdoms of the world we live in? First, we should have no delusions about the character and nature of these other kingdoms. According to Jesus and the New Testament, Satan and other hostile spiritual powers exercise authority in our current world system.[15] That is why the kingdoms are characterized by pride and violence. Second, we should understand that God "uses governments as he finds them, in all their ungodly rebellious ways, to serve his own providential purposes."[16] Human governments have no intrinsic metaphysical value, but God uses human governments to maintain relative measures of tranquility and justice, or at least to keep order.[17] That is why we pray for "kings and all those who are in authority."[18] Third, we should not forget the church and not human government is the focus of God's sovereign rule.[19] God uses the church to carry out the ultimate

---

[14] Boyd, *The Myth of a Christian Nation*, 30.

[15] Matthew 4:8–9; John 12:31; Romans 8:35–39.

[16] Boyd, *The Myth of a Christian Nation*, 20.

[17] Yoder, *The Christian Witness in the State*, 12–13.

[18] 1 Timothy 2:2–4. "God's will is that we should be able to live quiet and godly lives. The duty of government before God is to permit this" (Yoder, *He Came Preaching Peace*, 27).

[19] Colossians 1:13–20; Yoder, *The Christian Witness in the State*, 8–13.

purpose of history: proclaiming the gospel of the Kingdom, being the presence of the Kingdom, and participating in God's mission to make all things new.[20]

Given the nature of politics, the church must be on guard against the idolatry of political ideologies.[21] For example, the so-called Christian Right embraces and advocates a conservative political ideology. This ideology encompasses many good and compelling ideas, including limited government, personal liberty and responsibility, and the protection of unborn human life. But there is a fundamental flaw. The kingdom of God is not about conserving the status quo, or about restoring the idealized status quo of a previous generation. The kingdom of God is always a loving assault on the status quo, because—by definition—the status quo is always an expression of the bogus world system.

The so-called Christian Left has emerged to counter the so-called Christian Right. This seems to be a case in which the purported cure is worse than the disease. The so-called Christian Left embraces and advocates a progressive political ideology. This ideology encompasses many commendable ideals, including collective responsibility for the poor and for the environment. But there is a fundamental flaw. Progressive ideology puts hope and confidence in the coercive power of human government. This ideology does not believe that human governments exist merely for the purpose of keeping order. Rather, the ideologically progressive government aspires to solve every human problem (ranging from poverty to childhood obesity) by state action. John Howard

---

[20] Yoder, *The Christian Witness in the State*, 10–11.

[21] "The life of a Christian is characterized ... by the renunciation of any kind of ideology in the name of Christianity" (Rahner, *Foundations of Christian Faith*, 402).

Ideology

Yoder's comments about this aspiration are right on point: "The more a state aspires to a higher mission, a semi-religious role or one designed to control world history, whether in the west or in the east, the more the Christian will become suspicious with respect to the state."[22] N. T. Wright critiques progressive ideology, which he calls the "myth of progress," a "Utopian dream [that] is a parody of the Christian vision."[23] The bottom line is that the kingdom of God is not progressive. It does not evolve or erupt through political strategy, insurrection, or legislation. No, the kingdom of God irrupts; it breaks into history through the cruciform love of the Liberating King and his church.

There are substantive biblical reasons, therefore, to question certain aspects and assumptions of both conservative and progressive political ideologies. The more basic problem, however, may be the way political ideologies distract us from the mission and thereby compromise our witness. Specifically, political ideologies tend to promote and reinforce arrogance, not humility. If I believe that I have the blueprint for the best possible socioeconomic order, then I probably am not a humble person. I probably am not in touch with the fact that I do not know all of the variables and contingencies. I probably am not taking into account the pernicious impact of the law of unintended consequences. I probably am ignoring the catastrophic reality of sin in the bogus world system. Finally and fundamentally, I am not following the example and teaching of Jesus, who transcended the politics of this world by emptying himself, humbling himself, becoming a

---

[22] Yoder, *Discipleship as Political Responsibility*, 45.
[23] Wright, *Surprised by Hope*, 82.

slave, and allowing himself to be crucified for the sake of others and for the glory of God.

In addition, political ideologies tend to promote meanness. I am not referring here to the demonic violence of genocide or mass murder perpetrated by both left- and right-wing regimes in the twentieth century. Rather, I am referring to the mean-spirited way that people with one ideological perspective routinely attack people with a competing ideological perspective. If—based on my ideology—I am convinced beyond a reasonable doubt that I am right about a political issue or agenda, and—based on your ideology—you disagree with me, then I may be predisposed to dismiss you as an ignorant dupe or assail your motives or your character by calling you a racist, or a xenophobe, or some other politicized invective. Either way, I would be breaching my duty to walk in humility, which requires me to get rid of "bitterness, anger, wrath, insult and slander" and to "be kind and compassionate" to my brothers and sisters, loving them just as God has loved me.[24]

Jesus was not apolitical, and he has not called us to be apolitical. Rather, he calls us to a radically and qualitatively different type of politics: the politics of discipleship, of faithfulness to the Liberating King. The politics of Jesus are not based on efficiency or expediency, or any utilitarian calculus about ends justifying means. In humility, we put no confidence in the political ideologies of the bogus world system; we trust God to take care of the ends, and we prayerfully focus on the mission of the Kingdom by imitating the cruciform love of God.

---

[24] Ephesians 4:30—5:2.

Ideology

Father, free us from the idolatry of ideologies. Do not let your church—the bride of the Liberating King—become a handmaiden to any ideology or kingdom of the bogus world system. Forgive us for our pride and our meanness. Holy Spirit, empower us to be faithful to the politics of your kingdom. We pray that the shalom and justice of your kingdom will be present among us, and that through us, the world will know you. Amen.

CHAPTER 14

CELEBRITY

The American Christian subculture that emerged and flourished in the latter half of the twentieth century, and still persists in a somewhat fractured form today, is a type of bizarro world.[1] We have our own slightly mutated versions of just about everything pop culture has to offer: theme parks, night clubs, pop music, rock music, rap music, alternative music, stand-up comedy, improvisational comedy, performance art, media outlets, publishing companies, magazines, jewelry, fashions, retail outlets, personal injury lawyers, tattoo parlors, yoga instructors, biker gangs, personal trainers, life coaches, multi-level marketing schemes, video games, websites, bloggers, tweeters, hipsters, fair trade coffee shops, and art galleries ... and celebrities relating to all of the above.

---

[1] Bizarro (also known as "Htrae") is a fictional planet in the DC Comics universe inhabited by bizarro versions of Superman, Lois Lane, and other DC characters.

Celebrity

Christian celebrities engage the services of Christian public relations firms to help them manage their public images and market their products. I wish that I was making this up, but I am not. One of my best friends worked for one of these firms. She represented some of the biggest names in the American Christian subculture. Based on my conversations with her, I am convinced that the pursuit and preservation of so-called Christian fame is hard to reconcile with the call to cruciform humility.

The basic problem is the irreconcilable tension between trying to please people and trying to please God. This tension is not new. In his first letter to the Thessalonians, Paul described his ministry in the following terms:

> For we haven't approached you—or anyone else for that matter—with some error or impure motives or deceitful agenda, but as we have been approved by God and entrusted with the good news, that's how we are telling the world. We aren't trying to please everybody, but God, the only One who can truly examine our motives. As you know, we didn't sandwich the truth between cunning compliments—we told it straight—and before the eye of God, we never conspired to make a single cent off of you. We didn't come seeking respect from people—not from you or anyone else—although we could have leveraged our position as emissaries of the Anointed One, the Liberating King.[2]

Paul contrasts his motives, methods, and goals with those who 1) are motivated by monetary gain, and 2) use flattering speech, in order to 3) please people and be glorified by people, and to 4) get paid by people. Paul wants nothing to do with these hucksters

---

[2] 1 Thessalonians 2:3–6 (*The Voice*).

because he understands that: 1) the gospel is a sacred trust that gives rise to a fiduciary duty, and 2) he cannot fool God, who examines our hearts.

In First Corinthians, Paul points out another problem with celebrity status: it opens the door to factions based on allegiances to notable personalities—

> My brothers and sisters, I urge you by the name of our Lord [and Savior, Jesus], to come together in agreement. Do not allow anything or anyone to create division among you. Instead, be restored, completely fastened together with one mind and shared judgment. I have heard troubling reports from Chloe's people that you, my siblings, are consumed by fighting and petty disagreements. What I have heard is that each of you is taking sides, saying "I am with Paul," or "I am with Apollos," or "I am with Cephas," or "I am with the [Liberator]."[3]

There is, of course, an obvious problem with putting too much stock in celebrity leaders. They are scandal prone, and their scandals are newsworthy because of their high profile. Of course, people who are hostile and/or skeptical about the gospel use each new scandal as a pretext to ignore or dismiss Jesus. "The bigger they are, the harder they fall" is a trustworthy saying. When Christian celebrities fall, the collateral damage can be devastating.

A careful reading of Paul's letters indicates that he made a conscious effort to avoid the pitfalls of fame. He did not rely on flashy presentations or "brilliance of speech";[4] he kept his "day job" as a tentmaker because he "did not want to be a financial

---

[3] 1 Corinthians 1:10–12 (*The Voice*).

[4] 1 Corinthians 2:1.

burden";[5] he did not isolate himself from regular people, but developed deep personal friendships everywhere he went;[6] and he made sure that Jesus always was the main attraction.[7] In sum, Paul made sure that his ministry was not about himself. He did not cultivate a public image, or try to put anything over on anybody. He lived his life with a constant awareness that "God is not mocked."[8]

Paul no doubt did what he did because he knew where Jesus stood on the issue. In Matthew 23, Jesus pulls no rhetorical punches in his criticism of religious leaders who seek and enjoy public acclaim:

> They are interested, above all, in presentation: they wrap their heads and arms in the accoutrements of prayer, they cloak themselves with flowing tassled prayer garments, they covet the seats of honor at fine banquets and in the synagogue, and they love it when people recognize them in the market place, call them "Teacher" and beam at them.[9]

Jesus expresses utter and complete contempt for religious showoffs, who abuse their positions of trust to get perks, and who take inordinate pride in their titles and professional credentials. Jesus warns His followers that they must avoid the prideful practices of the Pharisees and scribes:

---

[5] 1 Thessalonians 2:9.
[6] Philemon 1:9–10.
[7] 1 Corinthians 2:2.
[8] Galatians 6:7.
[9] Matthew 23:5–7 (*The Voice*).

Do not let anyone call you "Rabbi," that is, "Teacher." For you are all brothers, and you have only one teacher . . . Indeed, do not call anyone on Earth "Father," for you have only one father, and He is in heaven. Neither let anyone call you "leader," for you have one leader—[the Liberating King]. If you are recognized at all, let it be for your service. Delight in the one who calls you servant. [Delight in the one who does not notice you at all.] For whoever exalts himself will be humbled, and whoever humbles himself will be exalted.[10]

Given the strong words of Jesus, and the example of Paul, I am not sure how or why any Christian leader or preacher could think it is a good idea to put his face on a billboard. It is one thing to die on a cross. It is another thing to pursue fame and fortune by talking about a humble man who suffered and died on a cross.

Jesus makes it clear that there are no big shots in his kingdom, at least for now. Ultimately, when the Kingdom is fully consummated, some will be exalted. Humility is the sole criterion he will use to decide who is exalted. This is a strong word to all who aspire to be big shots now, and particularly to those who actually obtain some measure of celebrity in the bizarro Christian subculture. Those who will be recognized as great in the Kingdom probably are not famous now; those who will be recognized as great in the Kingdom probably are serving in relative obscurity in distinctly unglamorous ways.

I have been blessed to know a few people who may be recognized as great in the Kingdom. A few years ago, I was privileged to speak at the funeral of one of my former legal secretaries. Her name was Sue (which is a great name for a legal secretary),

---

[10] Matthew 23:8–12 (*The Voice*).

and—frankly—she was not a very good secretary. She had all of the requisite skills, and she was fiercely loyal, but she often was away from her desk. Sue was a smoker. She had been a smoker long before she became a follower of Jesus, and she never could kick the habit. She always was a bit embarrassed by this failure, but God was pleased to use her smoking to advance his kingdom.

Every day, several times a day, she would get on the elevator from our offices near the top of a downtown skyscraper, and she would go to the street to smoke. She never went alone. Jesus went with her. Other smokers went with her too. Over the years, during these often extended smoke breaks, Sue—in a very natural and direct but nonconfrontational way, talked to her fellow smokers about Jesus. Many of them responded to the Good News. A lot of them were at the funeral. As I stood in front of the church, and considered the impact of one unheralded nicotine-addicted herald, I wept, and I am weeping right now as I think about it.

This is the beauty of the Kingdom. While we tend to focus on the gifts and foibles of great and famous celebrities, the Kingdom advances through good and faithful servants.

Lord, help us to avoid the pitfalls of the bizarro Christian subculture. Teach us the way of humble, self-effacing service that pleases you. Amen.

CHAPTER 15

BRAVERY

I was not raised in a God-fearing, churchgoing family. Depending on the season, Sundays were for yard work, hunting, batting practice, or golf. When it was not deer season or baseball season, my dad used to take me to play golf at a course called the Red Barn Par Three. He took me there because my violent and ineffective golf swing was not ready for the country club. The Red Barn was not a classy course. You didn't have to wear a shirt with a collar. In fact, you didn't even have to wear a shirt. In the snack bar at the Red Barn, next to a picture of John Wayne, there was a hand-lettered sign that made a big impression on me: "Yea though I walk through the valley of the shadow of death, I shall fear no evil because I am the meanest son of a bitch in the valley." I loved that sign. So did my dad.

My dad always stressed the need to be tough, to not back down. He made sure that I had rudimentary fighting skills, and he was proud when I used those skills, provided that I did not *start* the fight. I was pretty sure that my dad—a World War II veteran—was not afraid of anybody or anything. That is the way I wanted to be too—one of many unrealistic personal goals.

As I got a bit older, I realized that everybody has fears. Some people hide their fears well, and some people don't; some people are able to overcome their fears, and some people can't. Some people show amazing courage, but nobody is 100 percent fearless. I also realized that there is a significant difference between temerity (defined as "foolish boldness" or "recklessness") and bravery or courage. The sign at the Red Barn snack bar was an expression of temerity. I am pretty sure that the guy who conceived and produced the sign was in serious denial about the harsh realities of "the valley of the shadow of death." But the poet who wrote Psalm 23 knew those harsh realities very well.

Psalm 23 was written by David, a shepherd who became a celebrity by taking on Goliath, the champion of the Philistine armies. The confrontation took place in the Valley of Elah. Goliath stood in the valley and taunted the men who were assembled to defend Israel: "I defy the ranks of Israel this day; give me a man that we may fight together."[1] There were no takers. Saul and his men were "dismayed and greatly afraid" because Goliath was a huge man, protected by "scale armor which weighed 5000 shekels of bronze," and brandishing multiple weapons, including a spear that weighed "600 shekels of iron."[2] David was not one of Saul's fighting men. His dad sent him to the camp to deliver some food for his brothers. When David heard Goliath taunting the men of Israel, and realized that no one was stepping up to meet his challenge, David persuaded Saul to let him represent Israel

---

[1] 1 Samuel 17:10.
[2] 1 Samuel 17:4–7.

against the Philistine champion. After pointing out that David was completely unqualified for the mission, a reticent Saul said to David, "Go, and may YHWH be with you."[3] That, of course, was the key to David's bravery.

David walked into the valley with no armor, sword, or spear. He had a stick, a sling, and five smooth stones. It was an absurd scene. Goliath was disappointed and insulted that Israel had sent an obviously unqualified and ill-equipped opponent. Nonetheless, Goliath cursed David, and prepared to kill him. David responded: "You come to me with a sword, a spear, and a javelin, but I come to you in the name of YHWH of hosts, the God of the armies of Israel, whom you have taunted."[4] David explained his theocentric battle plan: "This day YHWH will deliver you into my hands . . . [so that everybody may know] . . . that YHWH does not deliver by sword or spear; for the battle belongs to YHWH."[5]

This was a classic confrontation between temerity and bravery. Based on appearances, David was the one with temerity. It seemed to be an act of foolish boldness to take on Goliath with a sling and a few rocks; but appearances can be misleading. As the narrative progresses, it becomes clear that David acted with courage because he knew that YHWH was with him, and Goliath—with misplaced confidence in his size, strength, skills, armor, weapons, and reputation—acted with foolish boldness when he challenged the faithful servant of YHWH.

Later, David writes about his experience: "YHWH is my shepherd." Psalm 23 is not a poem by a proud champion. It is a humble

---

[3] 1 Samuel 17:37.
[4] 1 Samuel 17:45.
[5] 1 Samuel 17:47.

tribute to YHWH, the ultimate provider and protector. Sometimes YHWH's faithfulness is experienced in "green pastures" beside "quiet waters." Other times, the setting is very different. "Even though I walk through the valley of the shadow of death, I fear no evil, for you are with me." It is impossible to miss the nexus between these words and the confrontation in the Valley of Elah. David's courage was not based on being the "meanest son of a bitch in the valley"; that title clearly belonged to Goliath. David had no fear because he knew YHWH, and he knew that YHWH was with him in the struggle.

This is the life that God offers to his people. In this broken and rebellious world, we walk in the valley of the shadow of death, but God calls us to live without fear. In the Hebrew Scripture the phrase "do not be afraid" (or "have no fear") appears over fifty times. Typically, the command is tied to YHWH's promise to protect and vindicate his people. For example, in Isaiah 7, two kings combined their forces and attacked Jerusalem. YHWH sent Isaiah to deliver a message to Ahaz, King of Judah: "Take care, be calm, have no fear, and do not be fainthearted."[6] These commands would be empty rhetoric if Ahaz's prospects were contingent on conventional military tactics or weapons. Without YHWH, Judah could not prevail; with YHWH, Judah had nothing to fear. The call to fearlessness is grounded in YHWH's faithfulness.

This fundamental principle of courage is evident in the amazing story of Shadrach, Meshach, and Abednego.[7] A corrupt king had demanded a kind of worship that these young Jewish men knew they could not give. And so they were required to face

---

[6] Isaiah 7:4.
[7] Daniel 3.

a fiery death in a blazing furnace. Most of us are quite familiar with the outcome. God showed up in a miraculous way to rescue them that day; but there is something also so powerful about the humility they showed before they courageously walked into that fire. They addressed the king and said, "O Nebuchadnezzar, we do not need to defend ourselves before you in this matter. If we are thrown in the blazing furnace, the God we serve is able to save us from it, and he will rescue us from your hand, O king. But even if he does not, we want you to know, O king, that we will not serve your gods or worship the image of gold you have set up."[8] Those young men understood that they served a God capable of re-ordering the natural world, but their faithfulness was not contingent on any presumption regarding a miraculous rescue. In humble acquiescence to his authority, they chose fealty and acted bravely.

Jesus reiterates this principle in his proclamation of the kingdom of God. For example, in Luke 12, Jesus suggests that his followers may face violent opposition and persecution, but commands them not to "fear those who kill the body."[9] Jesus, possibly alluding to Psalm 23, says, "Fear not, little flock, because your Father delights to give you his kingdom."[10] In John 14, Jesus is preparing his friends for his departure. He knows that hard times are coming. He gives them shalom, and tells them that their hearts "must not be troubled or fearful."[11] In John 16, he puts the

---

[8] Daniel 3:16–18.
[9] Luke 12:4.
[10] Luke 12:32.
[11] John 14:27.

directive in positive terms: "Be courageous! I have overcome the bogus world system."[12]

As predicted by Jesus, his followers faced persecution and suffering. For that reason, the call to courage was reiterated. For example, in Hebrews, the author is exhorting the readers to persevere in spite of opposition. He reminds them that God is with them, and will never abandon them. Then he quotes Psalm 118: "YHWH is my helper. I will not be afraid. What can man do to me?"[13] In Romans, Paul assures his brothers and sisters that they need not fear tribulation, persecution, peril, sword, death, or any hostile powers because "God is for us" and "nothing can separate us from the love of God."[14] In Revelation, the church at Smyrna is facing persecution. Some of the brothers are being thrown into prison. Jesus tells John to write these words to his people in Smyrna: "Don't be afraid of what you are about to suffer . . . Be faithful unto death, and I will give you the crown of life."[15]

All of this is good in theory. It seems self-evident that the Scriptures repeatedly tell us not to fear because the message is contrary to our natural and persistent inclination to live in and by fear. A case in point is Timothy, one of the heroes of the New Testament. He travelled with his friend and mentor Paul, and he often took on tough assignments. At one point, Paul left him to serve in Ephesus, where he had to deal with an array of false teachers, busybodies, slackers, and profiteers. Subsequently, Paul was thrown in prison (again). The circumstances were

---

[12] John 16.33.
[13] Hebrews 13:5–6.
[14] Romans 8:35–39.
[15] Revelation 2:10.

discouraging. Paul sensed that Timothy was reeling, and wrote to encourage him:

> Therefore, I remind you to keep ablaze the gift of God that is in you through the laying on my hands. For God has not given us a Spirit of fear, but of power, love, and sound judgment.[16]

These are very strong words from Paul. The implication is that Timothy had forgotten the source of courage, the Holy Spirit, God's empowering presence.[17] Timothy may have been trying to manage the problems at Ephesus by relying on his own experience, reputation, connections, and credentials, rather than by humbly surrendering to the Spirit and finding strength in God's grace. If that was the case, then Timothy was acting with temerity, because it is foolish boldness to try to lead God's people and preach the gospel without relying on God's power. I know this from painful personal experience. In 1983, I was hired by Young Life to start a new ministry in Clear Lake, a suburban community southeast of Houston. I had no doubt that I was the right guy for the job. As a volunteer Young Life leader in college and seminary, I had a track record of success. I was not surprised by my success because I knew that I had the essential skills and qualifications for being a Young Life leader: I was funny; I had an advanced degree in theology; I had a background in law enforcement and rugby; I had song-leading skills, pie-throwing skills, nunchuck skills, bow hunting skills . . . did I mention that I thought I was funny? I expected to take the community by storm. During my first few months in Clear Lake, things did not go according to

---

[16] 2 Timothy 1:6–7.

[17] Fee, *God's Empowering Presence*, 785–89.

my plan. I tried every trick in the book to create momentum for the ministry, but my efforts were thwarted by a bewildering and demoralizing combination of opposition and indifference. Some kids and their parents were sure that I was a cult leader; others were sure that I was completely irrelevant. My skills were useless. After an entire semester of very hard work, only two kids came to our last meeting before Christmas break, and one of them had to be there because the meeting was at her house. I viewed my ministry as a failure, which made me a failure. My self-confidence was obliterated. I was ready to quit. I try not to forget what I learned the hard way: temerity in ministry produces no fruit; pride-fueled "confidence in the flesh" produces only frustration and a sense of futility. Ultimately, temerity gives way to timidity or cowardice, which has nothing to do with humility.

This brings us to the paradox of biblical bravery. We can live without fear only if we live in fear. The biblical imperatives not to fear the opposition of people or hostile spiritual powers are predicated on the biblical imperative to fear God. This is not the kind of fear that causes avoidance. This is the reverent awe that causes grateful humility, worship, and obedience. If a man does not fear God, that means he does not really know the living and true God—the King of kings and Lord of lords, the judge of all, the consuming fire, who is with us and for us, and from whose love nothing can separate us. If a man does not know and fear God, then he will not be inclined to humbly submit to God.[18] If a man does not humbly submit to God, then he will not have the

---

[18] The Rule of Benedict States that "the first desire of humility" is "that a person should keep the fear of God before his eyes and beware of ever foregoing it" (www.osb.org/rb/text).

courage that only God can provide, and he will become a hostage of the fearsome realities of the corrupt world system. This is our daily choice. We can fear God, be humble, and live bravely as beneficiaries and agents of his kingdom. Or we can put our confidence in the flesh, sometimes acting with temerity, sometimes lapsing into timidity, never quite shaking the chronic and debilitating fears that dominate life in the bogus world system.

God, teach us to fear you—and to fear nothing or no one else. Jesus, thank you for demonstrating humble bravery on the cross. Holy Spirit, empower us for courageous service.

CHAPTER 16

MORTALITY

My friend Mark died in 1973. He was a high school senior. He was with some buddies on a Friday night. They were going to kidnap a rival school's mascot, a goofy, oversized icon of a Confederate general holding a sword. Mark had a heart attack in David's car. He died in the hospital emergency room. I found out a few hours later when David showed up at my door. The funeral was a few days later. David and I were pallbearers. The service was at a Unitarian church. The pastor read the following words:

> All mankind is of one author, and is one volume; when one man dies, one chapter is not torn out of the book, but translated into a better language; and every chapter must be so translated . . . As therefore the bell that rings to a sermon, calls not upon the preacher only, but upon the congregation to come: so this bell calls us all; but how much more me, who am brought so near the door by this sickness . . . No man is an island, entire of

itself... any man's death diminishes me, because I am involved in mankind; and therefore never send to know for whom the bell tolls; it tolls for thee."[1]

Mark was buried at a cemetery on the edge of town. I rode with David to the cemetery. After we threw some dirt on Mark's coffin, we left. David drove close to one hundred miles per hour, changing lanes aggressively, recklessly. I was riding shotgun without a seat belt. I didn't care.

I had accepted Jesus into my heart a few months before Mark died. I still was a bit fuzzy on what that meant, but I knew that I was supposed to talk to Jesus about people and talk to people about Jesus. I stopped doing both for several months after Mark died. I assumed that God was responsible for death in general, and for Mark's death in particular. I cut off communications as a protest.

Since 1973, I have attended and participated in too many funerals for young people. That is one of the sad and bewildering consequences of being a Young Life leader for several decades. Often I have been called upon to speak for God—or about God—in these tragic circumstances. I don't have much to say to grieving parents, siblings, and friends. I point to Jesus, weeping at the tomb of his friend Lazarus; I point to Jesus, tasting death on a Roman cross; and then I point to the empty tomb.

Over the years, through seasons of prayer and study, struggling to resist the temptations of rage and resignation, I have learned to embrace mortality with humility, but to view death as an enemy.

---

[1] John Donne, "Meditation XVII."

Mortality

According to Scripture, there is a causal nexus between sin and death. "Sin entered the world through one man, and death through sin, and in this way, death came to all people, because all sinned."[2] This verse, of course, summarizes the tragic sequence of events in the Garden of Eden. Adam and Eve, created in God's image and animated by God's breath, lived in, tended to, and benefitted from God's garden. The ultimate benefit and blessing of the garden was fellowship with God, which is the essence of life.[3] That fellowship was contingent on man's humility, expressed as dependent fidelity.[4]

One day, the tempter approached Eve, asked her a theological question ("Did God really say . . . ?"), invited Eve to consider the possibility that God had imposed unreasonable restrictions on her rights, lied to her ("You will not surely die"), and convinced her to exalt herself ("You will be like God . . .") through an autonomous act of defiance.[5] Eve, and then Adam, rejected the way of humility and chose the path of pride, with calamitous consequences. The most calamitous of those calamitous consequences is death: "For dust you are and to dust you will return."[6]

This is what it means to be mortal. We are subject to the imperative of death. We must die, "earth to earth, ashes to ashes, dust to dust."[7] Shakespeare observed, "Golden lads and girls all must / as

---

[2] Romans 5:12.

[3] Vos, *Biblical Theology*, 27.

[4] Ibid., 32.

[5] Ibid., 34–38; Genesis 3:1–7

[6] Genesis 3:19.

[7] This phrase from the traditional English Burial Service dates back to the 1662 version of the Book of Common Prayer.

chimney sweepers, come to dust."[8] Hank Williams lamented, "No matter how much I struggle and strive / I'll never get out of this world alive."[9] This raw fact should promote a measure of humility, but our narcissism recoils against it. Ernest Becker describes this phenomenon in Freudian terms:

> Freud discovered that each of us repeats the tragedy of the mythical Greek Narcissus: we are hopelessly absorbed with ourselves. If we care about anyone, it is usually with ourselves first of all. Aristotle somewhere put it: luck is when the guy next to you gets hit with the arrow. Twenty-five hundred years of history have not changed man's basic narcissism; most of the time, for most of us, this is still a workable definition of luck. It is one of the meaner aspects of narcissism that we feel practically everyone is expendable except ourselves . . . This narcissism is what keeps men marching into point-blank fire in wars: at heart one doesn't feel he will die, he only feels sorry for the man next to him. Freud's explanation for this is that the unconscious does not know death or time: in man's physiochemical, inner organic recesses, he feels immortal.[10]

Putting aside the ponderous Freudian lexicon, and without embracing Freud's pseudo-scientific explanation, Becker's basic point is well-taken. Just as our pride leads to death, our narcissism leads to the denial of death, or at least the attempted denial

---

[8] William Shakespeare, *Cymbeline*, Act IV.

[9] This was the last single to be released during Hank Williams's lifetime. The song reached #1 on the Billboard Country Singles chart a few days after his death, at age 29.

[10] Becker, *The Denial of Death*, 2.

of death. But we cannot change who we are and what we are. We are created in the image of God, but—as a consequence of our sin—we are dust destined for dust. Becker, inspired in part by Kierkegaard's contemplation of our "creatureliness," calls us self-conscious animals:

> What does it mean to be a self-conscious animal? The idea is ludicrous, if it is not monstrous. It means to know that one is food for worms. This is the terror: to have emerged from nothing, to have a name, conscious of self, deep inner feelings, an excruciating inner yearning for life and self-expression—and with all this yet to die.[11]

In *O, Death*, Ralph Stanley sings about this terror. In this haunting song, we hear a conversation between a desperate man and a relentless and confident adversary, death:

> O, Death
> O, Death
>
> Won't you spare me over 'til another year
> Well what is this that I can't see
> With ice cold hands takin' hold of me
> Well I am death, none can excel
> I'll open the door to heaven or hell
> Whoa, death someone would pray
> Could you wait to call me another day
> The children prayed, the preacher preached
> Time and mercy is out of your reach

---

[11] Ibid., 87.

Get Low

I'll fix your feet 'til you can't walk
I'll lock your jaw 'til you can't talk
I'll close your eyes so you can't see
This very air, come and go with me
I'm death I come to take the soul
Leave the body and leave it cold
To draw up the flesh off of the frame
Dirt and worm both have a claim

O, Death
O, Death

Won't you spare me over 'til another year
My mother came to my bed
Placed a cold towel upon my head
My head is warm my feet are cold
Death is a-movin' upon my soul
Oh, death how you're treatin' me
You've closed my eyes so I can't see
Well you're hurtin' my body
You make me cold
You run my life right outta my soul
Oh death please consider my age
Please don't take me at this stage
My wealth is all at your command
If you will move your icy hand
Oh the young, the rich or poor
Hunger like me you know
No wealth, no ruin, no silver no gold
Nothing satisfies me but your soul

> O, Death
> O, Death
>
> Won't you spare me over 'til another year
> Won't you spare me over 'til another year
> Won't you spare me over 'til another year.[12]

How do we move beyond the terror of death? First, we confront the reality of death—we contemplate mortality to cultivate humility. In an Ash Wednesday essay, Dan Clendenin notes that the "counsel to 'remember death' was standard wisdom for the early church fathers:"

> Gregory of Nazianzus (329–388) echoed Plato when he suggested that our present life ought to be "a meditation upon death." He advised his friend Philagrios to live "instead of the present the future, and to make this life a meditation and practice of death." To the priest Photios he wrote: "Our cares and our attention are concentrated on one thing only, our departure from this world. For this departure we prepare ourselves and gather our baggage as prudent travelers would do." In his treatise *On Virginity*, Athanasius (296–373) encouraged readers to "recall your exodus every hour, keep death before your eyes on a daily basis. Remember before whom you must appear." John Climacus (525–605) advised us to "let the memory of death

---

[12] Ralph Stanley, "O Death," *O Brother, Where Art Thou?* (Mercury Records, 2000).

sleep and awake with you." So too St. Benedict, who in his Rule (c 530) advised his monks to "set death before one's self daily."[13]

As we contemplate our mortality, we shed the narcissism of denial, and we expose the folly of the "boastful pride of life."[14] We remember that we are dust, with no bragging rights, no guarantee of one more day, or even one more minute. This perspective will help us resist the lies of the tempter, and to live in dependent fidelity towards our Liberator. This perspective will help us to remember that our only hope is Jesus, who is the Resurrection and the Life. If we belong to Jesus, "to die is to gain."[15]

The disciplined contemplation of mortality also prepares us to die well, and to serve others as they prepare to die well. In previous generations, the tradition of *ars moriendi* (the art of dying) provided spiritual and practical guidance of the moribund and their loved ones.[16] Today, too often, we move quickly from denial to despair, we outsource the dying process to professionals, and we miss sacred opportunities for worship and service. Dying well has become a lost art.[17]

---

[13] Dan Clendenin, "Meditation on Mortality," www.journeywithjesus.net/essays.

[14] 1 John 2:16.

[15] Philippians 1:21.

[16] Faust, *The Republic of Suffering*, 10. "The Art of Dying" (*Ars Moriendi*) is a Latin text dating from the fifteenth century which explained the type of behaviors and protocols that determine a "good death."

[17] There are, of course, notable exceptions. On July 27, 2011, John Stott—faithful pastor, prolific author, wise theologian, winsome ambassador—died at the age of 90. His last few weeks were very painful, but he was surrounded by family and friends. When he died, he was listening to Handel's *Messiah*,

As we contemplate the reality of mortality, however, we must not capitulate to the reign of death; we must never forget that the way things are—specifically including the syndrome of sin and death—is not the way things ought to be, or ultimately will be. "Man rightly follows the intuition of his heart when he abhors and repudiates the absolute ruin and total disappearance of his own person. Man rebels against death because he bears in himself an eternal seed which cannot be reduced to mere matter."[18]

The New Testament is not ambiguous on this point: death is not God's ally or agent; death is a hostile power, an enemy, "not a good part of the good creation."[19] In fact, death is the last enemy to be humbled and destroyed.[20] In the ultimate victory, the One who is the Resurrection and the Life will transform our bodies of dust, clothing the perishable with the imperishable, "the mortal with immortality," and death will be "swallowed up in victory."[21] In the "new heaven and new earth," there will be "no more death or mourning or crying or pain."[22] At that time, the rescued ones will celebrate the triumph of the Liberating King and the death of death: "Where, O death, is your victory? Where, O death, is your sting?"[23]

---

and his friends were reading to him from the Bible ("John Stott Has Died," www.christianitytoday.com).

[18] Wojtyla, *The Gospel of Life*, 122 (quoting the Second Vatican Council).

[19] Wright, *Surprised by Hope*, 99.

[20] 1 Corinthians 15:26.

[21] 1 Corinthians 15:53–54. Paul is so confident of the outcome that he sometimes speaks of the destruction of death as an accomplished fact (see 2 Timothy 1:10).

[22] Revelation 21:4.

[23] 1 Corinthians 15:55.

Until that day, we groan in our "earthly tents" as we long for our "heavenly dwellings," and we grieve, but not like those who "have no hope."[24] However, we are not—in the words of Townes Van Zandt, "waiting around to die."[25] Rather, we are pressing on "toward the goal to win the prize,"[26] and to obtain the "kingdom that cannot be shaken."[27] As we pass through seasons of deep pain, we speak truth to our enemy, "Death be not proud . . . Death thou shalt die,"[28] and we cast aside all vestiges of self-sufficiency, finding security only in the arms of the "Father of compassion and the God of all comfort."[29]

Father, give us the humility to remember that we are dust, the wisdom to know that our only hope is you, the power to live as resurrection people in the broken and rebellious bogus world system, and holy tenacity to proclaim your victory to those who are held hostage by the fear of death.

---

[24] 2 Corinthians 5:2; 1 Thessalonians 4:13.

[25] Townes Van Zandt, "Waiting Around to Die," *For the Sake of the Song* (Poppy Tomato, 1968).

[26] Philippians 3:14.

[27] Hebrews 12:28.

[28] John Donne, "Divine Sonnet X."

[29] 2 Corinthians 1:3.

CHAPTER 17

CHARITY

The King James Version of the Bible (KJV) translates 1 Corinthians 13:3 (in part) as follows: "And though I bestow all my goods to feed the poor ... and have not charity, it profiteth me nothing." That translation sometimes puzzles modern readers. We equate charity with the act of giving, but this translation suggests that a person can give sacrificially to a worthy cause without having charity.

The confusion arises because the KJV uses the English word charity to translate the Greek word *agape,* self-giving love. The English word charity derives from the Latin word *caritas,* but may be traced to another Greek word, *charis*—grace or gift.[1] The point of 1 Corinthians 13:4 is this: If I give to charity in an uncharitable (graceless) way, I have missed the mark of love. Jesus calls us to give out of humble gratitude, to give as people who have received grace.

---

[1] Thurston, *Religious Vows,* 34.

In the Kingdom Manifesto (Matthew 5—7), Jesus commented on charitable and uncharitable giving:

Part of imitating the perfection of God is acting charitably and generously, doing good deeds, working for justice and praying.
Jesus: But when you do these righteous acts, do not do them in front of spectators. Don't do them where you can be seen, let alone lauded, by others. If you do, you will have no reward from your Father in heaven. When you give to the poor, do not boast about it, announcing your donations with blaring trumpets as the play actors do. Do not brazenly give your charity in the synagogues and on the streets; indeed do not give at all, no, if you are giving because you want to be praised by your neighbors. Those people who give in order to reap praise have already received their reward.[2]

What can we say about the uncharitable giver? He may or may not care about the poor, but he definitely is giving to advance his own perceived self-interest. He is seeking praise or positive recognition from other people. That is why he makes sure to draw attention to his act of giving. That is pride, and—because of his pride—an uncharitable giver will have no reward in the Kingdom.

The charitable giver has a different *modus operandi*. He takes extreme measures to conceal his act of giving. He gives as a heartfelt expression of gratitude to God, who loves the poor and sees everything. Many people cultivate a secret life to hide shameful or embarrassing attitudes or habits, but Jesus' people are called to cultivate a secret life that is actually better than the life that is

---

[2] Matthew 6:2–4 (*The Voice*).

seen by other people. This is the way of Kingdom humility, and charitable giving is one manifestation of such humility.

In Second Corinthians, Paul provides additional insight into charitable giving. In context, he is talking about his effort to take up a collection for the poor in Jerusalem. Paul uses the word *charis* to characterize this project because the generosity of the Gentile churches towards their Jewish brothers and sisters in Jerusalem is "a sign of God's grace working itself out in their lives."[3]

For Paul, the paradigm of charitable giving—and the inspiration for the collection—is the *charis* of Jesus, who "though he was rich, yet for [our] sakes became poor, so that [we] through his poverty might become rich."[4] This statement is not primarily a comment on Jesus' financial situation, and it should not be taken as a promise of monetary wealth for anybody. Rather, this statement "sums up God's merciful action towards humanity."[5] Jesus indeed was "rich"; he pre-existed in indescribable glory as the *logos*, who, "in the beginning," was "with God" and "was God."[6] But he did not exploit this status for his own advantage. Instead, he became "poor"; he humbled himself in the self-giving, self-emptying downward mobility of incarnation and crucifixion. Paul's point is clear: "When we have been the beneficiaries of such undeserved grace, how can [we] shut [our] hearts or purses to brothers or sisters in need?"[7] With gratitude, we imitate the humility of God by giving to others.

---

[3] Garland, *2 Corinthians*, 388.
[4] 2 Corinthians 8:9.
[5] Garland, *2 Corinthians*, 376.
[6] John 1:1.
[7] Garland, *2 Corinthians*, 376.

Paul goes on to outline and discuss some of the principles of charitable giving. First, bountiful giving leads to bountiful blessings in God's kingdom.[8] The goal is to be rich towards God. It is a no-brainer to give up what we cannot keep (our money and our stuff) to get what we cannot lose (treasure in God's kingdom).

Second, we should not give as a result of coercion or compulsion.[9] In God's economy, it has to come from a heart that has been gripped by *charis*. A charitable giver gives with good cheer, even "hilarity."[10] This is one reason that some politicized theories of social justice miss the mark. The coercive redistribution of wealth by the taxing and police power of a human government in the bogus world system may or may not be good public policy, but it will not achieve the justice and equity of God's kingdom.

Third, we should give with the confidence that God is the ultimate giver.[11] He meets our needs. When we have more than we need, it is because he wants us to imitate the humility of Jesus by giving to those who lack.[12] Paul invokes the miracle of the manna to make this point: "He who gathered much did not have too much, and he who gathered little did not have too little."[13]

Fourth, we should give to glorify God, and to provoke thanksgiving to God.[14] The uncharitable giver seeks recognition and expects to be thanked as a benefactor. The charitable giver knows

---

[8] 2 Corinthians 9:6.
[9] 2 Corinthians 9:7.
[10] The Greek word is *hilarion*, typically translated as "cheerful."
[11] 2 Corinthians 9:8–10.
[12] 2 Corinthians 9:13–14.
[13] 2 Corinthians 9:15.
[14] 2 Corinthians 9:12.

that he gives as a beneficiary of *charis*. He wants people to join him in saying "thanks be to God for His indescribable gift."[15]

It is sobering to reflect on the way that we sometimes have ignored or distorted the teaching and example of Jesus. A lot of our giving is uncharitable giving. We routinely expect and receive (and sometimes even solicit) recognition and applause for our gifts. Christian universities and organizations call press conferences and issue press releases to announce big donations, and the big donors seem to relish the adulation. Churches tend to be slightly more subtle, but the same dynamic is evident; the left hand usually knows what the right hand is doing. It actually is surprising when somebody takes Jesus at his word by giving a significant gift anonymously, without strings or conditions. That is certainly the exception rather than the rule.

Uncharitable giving has been a chronic problem throughout church history. For example, consider the patrons who paid for the 12,000 square-foot mosaic floor of the Basilica Patriarcale Aquileia in the early fourth century:

> Leading members of the Christian community who donated money were publicly commemorated. Their portraits were carefully worked into the mosaics on the floor. Their smug, complacent stares still challenge the inquisitive stares of modern tourists. Nor were these self-satisfied Christians embarrassed to advertise their benefactions. The precise extent of their generosity is still plainly visible. A matter-of-fact inscription, again worked into the floor, records that "as a gift to God" the wealthy

---

[15] 2 Corinthians 9:15.

Januarius was responsible for financing "880 square feet" of mosaic. In Aquileia, there were no anonymous donors.[16]

Many years ago, I was a recipient of a generous gift. At the time, I was on Young Life staff, struggling to support my very young family. My struggle was compounded by the fact that I was one of the most hapless fund raisers in the history of Young Life. I failed to raise the budget, and was put on unpaid status for months at a time. Back in those days, Young Life would send paychecks for zero dollars. Each time one of those zero paychecks arrived in the mail, I felt like a complete failure, even though the ministry was impacting lots of kids. One day, I was called by a local banker. He told me that somebody had established an account for my family's benefit. Every month, an amount was deposited in the account. The money was enough to cover rent and groceries during the zero-paycheck months. I still don't know who gave the money, but I think about that gracious act all of the time. The person who funded that account was not advancing his or her self-interest in any way; there was no recognition, not even a tax deduction. The gift gave me a glimpse of the charity of the Kingdom, and I am confident that such charity will be rewarded by the King.

―――

Lord, forgive us for being proud uncharitable givers. Holy Spirit, touch our hearts with a deep sense of gratitude, teach us the way of Kingdom humility, and empower us to give as you have given. Thanks for Jesus, the indescribable gift. Amen.

---

[16] Kelly, *The End of Empire*, 258.

CHAPTER 18

IDOLATRY

The true gospel is always a loving assault on the status quo. In Thessalonica in the middle of the first century, the status quo was the Roman Empire, where Caesar claimed to be lord and savior, where patriotic subjects participated in the cult of the emperor, and where folks sought comfort, meaning, and community by celebrating a colorful array of gods and goddesses.[1] There were temples for Isis, goddess of fertility, Osiris, god of the dead, Cabirus, a local god of protection at sea, and Dionysus, the god of wine.[2] On a clear day, one could see Mount Olympus.

Paul came to Thessalonica after a wild adventure in Philippi, which featured a riot, a beating, an incarceration, an earthquake, and a number of conversions.[3] Actually, that was just another "day at the office" for Paul. Once he got to Thessalonica, Paul did

---

[1] Gorman, *Apostle of the Crucified Lord*, 146–47.
[2] Ibid.
[3] Acts 16:11–40.

what he always did. He proclaimed Jesus the Liberating King, and invited people to surrender to God's kingdom and glory. All kinds of people responded to this call. The defenders of the status quo launched a counterinsurgency, organizing a violent mob and accusing Paul of subverting Caesar by proclaiming another King.[4] Paul was accused of turning the world upside down.[5] That accusation was 100 percent correct.

However, Paul did not regard Caesar and his empire as the real enemy of God's kingdom. Paul understood that the real enemies of the Kingdom were hostile spiritual powers who worked in and through the status quo.[6] Paul called people in Thessalonica to join him in the struggle against those powers, and he laid out a radical action plan that is still in effect for the church today. The radical action plan is faith, love, and hope.

I know what you are thinking. This radical action plan does not sound radical. It sounds like a trite pious platitude that has been embroidered, painted, etched, stitched, and carved into a trillion semi-Christian knickknacks and consumer items, and —in recent years—probably has been tattooed in Latin or Greek on the scrawny torsos of a few good-hearted hipsters. That is a valid point, but when the dynamics of faith, love, and hope are properly understood, it is clear that we are not dealing with a banal slogan; faith, love, and hope are weapons of mass redemption in God's mission to make all things new.

---

[4] Acts 17:1–9.
[5] Acts 17:6.
[6] 1 Thessalonians 2:18; 3:5.

Idolatry

Paul was forced to leave Thessalonica abruptly, and he was concerned about his friends there.[7] He knew that they were facing persecution and social isolation because of their countercultural and counter-imperial allegiance to Jesus. He sent Timothy to see them, and Timothy reported back that they were keeping the faith. This report inspired Paul to write the letter known as First Thessalonians. That letter begins with an explosion of gratitude:

> We thank God for all of you, remembering you constantly in our prayers. We recall, in the presence of our God and Father, your work of faith, labor of love, and endurance of hope in our Lord Jesus the Liberating King, knowing your election, brothers and sisters loved by God. For our gospel did not come to you in word only, but also in power, in the Holy Spirit, and with full conviction. You know what kind of people we were among you for your benefit, and you became imitators of us and of the Lord when, in spite of severe persecution, you received the message with the joy of the Holy Spirit. As a result, you became an example to all the believers in Macedonia and Achaia. For the Lord's message rang out from you, not only in Macedonia and Achaia, but in every place that news of your faith from God has gone out, so we don't need to say anything. For they themselves report about us what kind of reception we had from you: How you turned to God from idols, to serve the living and true God, and to wait for his Son from heaven, whom he raised from the dead—Jesus, the one who rescues us from the wrath to come.[8]

---

[7] 1 Thessalonians 2:17—3:5.

[8] 1 Thessalonians 1:2–10.

There is a lot that can and should be said about this amazing passage. For example, we catch a glimpse of Paul's very intense prayer life, we are reminded of the distinction between empty rhetoric and supernatural power, and we learn something about contagious courage. For our present purpose, however, we will focus on the Thessalonian converts' three-pronged response to Paul's subversive gospel: they 1) turned to God from idols, for the purpose of 2) serving the living and true God, while they 3) wait for his Son from heaven.

The first prong is the "work of faith/faithfulness." The gospel is the story of Jesus' faithfulness, and the only appropriate response to that story is for us to go "all in" with faith by turning to God from idols.[9] For the Thessalonians, this meant that they had to turn from allegiance to false gods (Caesar, Isis, Osiris, and the rest) to the living and true God. This is a radical redirection, a complete 180 degree turn.

Years ago, as a result of a practical joke that got way out of hand, I became a police officer for the City of Dallas, Texas. That was a very educational experience. I picked up some cool skills, including pursuit driving skills. Because I was committed to excellence, and/or because I lacked impulse control, I tried to practice those skills everyday. The quintessential pursuit-driving skill may be the radical maneuver that reverses the direction of travel by 180 degrees in a minimum amount of time while staying within the width of a two-lane road. You have seen this maneuver in hundreds of high-quality movies. The car is driving fast in one direction, and suddenly it is driving almost as fast in the other direction. That maneuver is called a bootleg.

---

[9] Gorman, *Cruciformity*, 95–102 (describing our response of faith as the "fundamental option," a "total surrender of the self to God").

Idolatry

That is the way we are supposed to respond to Jesus. We are called to make a bootleg from the status quo (idolatry) to God. This is not accomplished by picking up Jesus as a hitchhiker and continuing on in generally the same direction with him in the passenger seat. This is only accomplished when we relinquish the wheel, surrender control. This, of course, requires humility, the recognition that Jesus is the more competent driver.

What does it look like for sophisticated people of the twenty-first century to turn from idols? It looks exactly the same as it did in the first century! There is nothing new under the sun. We still give our allegiance to multiple counterfeit gods, including Mammon (money), Eros (sex), Gnosis (knowledge), and Dynamis (power), but fundamentally we worship the bogus god of self. Jesus died on the cross to rescue us from this predicament: "He died for all so that those who live should live no longer for themselves, but for him who died for them and was raised."[10] Jesus died to rescue us from the futility and emptiness of idolatry, specifically including our pride-fueled impulse to put ourselves first.

The second prong of the Thessalonian response to Paul's subversive gospel is the "labor of love." We turn from idols in order to serve the living and true God. The word that is translated as labor typically denotes physical labor,[11] "blue collar" work rather than "white collar" work. The ultimate labor of love was Jesus' death on the cross, a distinctly physical endeavor that

---

[10] 2 Corinthians 5:15. The Rule of Benedict develops this fundamental theme: "The second degree of humility is that a person love not his own will nor take pleasure in satisfying his desires, but model his actions on the sayings of the Lord, 'I have not come to do My own will, but the will of Him who sent me.' (John 6:38)" (www.osb.org/rb/text).

[11] Fee, *The First and Second Letters to the Thessalonians*, 25–26.

involved some very heavy lifting and intense physical pain. We are called to love others the way that Jesus loved (and loves) us. We should be prepared, therefore, for heavy lifting—for practical acts of physical service. It is not sufficient to say "go in peace, keep warm, and eat well."[12] The service we are called to may require us to swing a hammer, cook a meal, dig a well, change a tire, or move a sleeper-sofa up three flights of stairs. The labor of love requires humble service.

The third prong is the "endurance of hope." We are waiting for the Son who will make all things new. Waiting is never easy. For those who have made a radical turn from the idols of the bogus world system, waiting requires the endurance that is made possible by hope. Hope in this context is not wishful thinking; it is confidence that God will do what he has promised to do.[13] In this broken and rebellious world, we are constantly tempted to give up on the self-denial of the Kingdom and give in to the self-gratification of the status quo. Paul was concerned that the tempter had tempted the Thessalonians to do that very thing,[14] but they had managed to resist because they did not lose hope. The essence of hope is humility, the recognition that only God's grace can sustain us, and that there is no hope in going our own way.[15]

Lord, we praise you because you are the one true God, the only one worthy of our devotion. Please give us the wisdom and the will to

---

[12] James 2:16 (this is given as the quintessential example of "dead faith").
[13] Ibid., 26.
[14] 1 Thessalonians 3:5.
[15] 1 Peter 1:13.

Idolatry

make that bootleg turn from idolatry to humility, so we can join you in the loving assault on the status quo, deploying faith, love, and hope, the weapons of mass redemption. Amen.

CHAPTER 19

AUTHORITY

When I was a younger man, I was not particularly deferential to authority or authority figures. That did not distinguish me from many of my contemporaries in the late 1960s and early 1970s. The bumper sticker on the VW bus said "Question Authority," so we did. Many of us were, to borrow a phrase from John Mellencamp, "acting out rebellion."[1] If someone asked us what we were rebelling against, we might mumble some drivel about "the Establishment." Or we might simply respond by quoting Marlon Brando's character from *The Wild One*, "Whaddya got?"

In our minds, Jesus was a heroic figure because he was a rebel, a non-conformist, an iconoclastic outsider. He was an advocate for love and peace, but he was willing to turn over a few tables in Herod's temple to make a point.[2] He certainly did not suck up to authority figures. Sometimes he gently made fun of them for

---

[1] John Mellencamp, "Authority Song," *Uh-huh* (Riva, 1984).
[2] Mark 11:15–16.

their pretensions and delusions,[3] and sometimes he harshly castigated them for their hypocrisy and abuse of power.[4] He rarely, if ever, had a kind word to say to them or about them. In a dramatic and climactic confrontation with Pilate, Jesus stood his ground, even as the chief priests and the temple police shouted "Crucify! Crucify!"[5] For aspiring rebels, Jesus seemed to be a good role model.

The rebel Jesus has been celebrated in protest songs, possibly starting with Woody Guthrie's song "Jesus Christ."[6] Guthrie was an iconic American folk singer. He rambled throughout the United States in the 1930s and 1940s, writing and collecting thousands of songs about coal miners, migrant workers, dust bowl refugees, and other folks struggling to get by in very hard times. According to Guthrie, Jesus was "A hard working man true and brave / [Who] said to the rich, 'Give your goods to the poor' / So they laid Jesus Christ in his grave."[7] Guthrie's Jesus was killed by bankers, preachers, cops, and soldiers because he was a threat to the rich, and Guthrie's Jesus looks forward to a day when the working people will rise up against the rich:

> When the love of the poor shall one day turn to hate
> When the patience of the workers gives away
> "Would be better for you rich if you never had been born"
> So they laid Jesus Christ in his grave.[8]

---

[3] Luke 22:25.
[4] Matthew 23:2–36.
[5] John 19:4–5.
[6] Woody Guthrie, "Jesus Christ" (www.elyrics.net).
[7] Ibid.
[8] Ibid.

Guthrie's version of Jesus may have been inspired in part by the Jesus of Scripture, but it is clear that Guthrie was using his version of Jesus to support his particular sociopolitical agenda.[9] Guthrie was not the first or the last person to engage in that type of revisionism.

In the early 1970s, Kris Kristofferson updated the message in "Jesus Was a Capricorn":

> Jesus was a Capricorn, he ate organic food
> He believed in love and peace and never wore no shoes
> Long hair, beard, and sandals and a funky bunch of friends
> Reckon they'd just nail him up if he came down again
> 'Cause everybody's got to have somebody to look down on
> Who they can feel better than at any time they please
> Someone doing something dirty decent folks can frown on
> If you can't find nobody else, just help yourself to me.[10]

With this song, Kristofferson is taking a shot at conservatives who assume that Jesus is on their side. Kristofferson suggests that Jesus has more in common with countercultural hippies than with ardent and sanctimonious defenders of the status quo. Kristofferson deploys his version of Jesus to defend his own

---

[9] In the introduction to Woody Guthrie's autobiography, *Bound for Glory*, Pete Seeger wrote: "In the desperate early Depression years, [Woody] developed a religious view of Christ, the Great Revolutionary" (quoted by Rob Collins, "Portrait of a Populist," www.woodyguthrie.org/merchandise/oklahomagazette.htm). According to Collins, Guthrie sympathized with many of the professed goals of the Communist Party, including the "redistribution of income," but he was never a member of the Communist Party (ibid.).

[10] Kris Kristofferson, "Jesus Was a Capricorn," *Jesus Was a Capricorn* (Monument Records, 1972).

refusal to conform to anybody else's standards or expectations. The last line of the chorus reveals that Kristofferson is proud of his own rebel persona: "If you can't find nobody else, just help yourself to me." That type of pride distinguishes the majority of self-proclaimed rebels from the rebel Jesus.

In the 1970s, Jackson Browne wrote a song called "Rebel Jesus." Browne's "Rebel Jesus" is a beautiful Christmas carol that critiques the way we celebrate Jesus' birthday:

> We guard our world with locks and guns
> We guard our fine possessions
> And once a year when Christmas comes
> We give to our relations
> And perhaps we give a little to the poor
> If the generosity should seize us
> But if anyone should interfere in the business
> Of why there are poor
> They get the same as the rebel Jesus.[11]

Browne's song suggests that Jesus was crucified because he challenged the structural reasons for poverty. Browne, a professed "pagan" and "heathen" with an impressive track record as a progressive activist, appeals to Jesus to support his political agenda, and reshapes the story of Jesus to fit his purpose. However, for reasons that Browne would probably reject, Browne's song may be heard in a way that is faithful to Jesus' mission. Specifically, Jesus' mission was (and is) to announce the irruption or invasion of the kingdom of God, which involves his triumph over

---

[11] Jackson Browne, "The Rebel Jesus," *Next Voice You Hear: The Best of Jackson Browne* (Elektra, 1977).

the hostile spiritual powers who work in and through the bogus world system.[12] Poverty is one of the symptoms of the dehumanizing power of sin. Jesus, therefore, definitely came to "interfere in the business of why there are poor." He was a rebel against the injustice of the bogus world system.

What does Scripture say about the rebel Jesus? He was not an anarchist. He did not reject all authority. He operated by and under the authority of the Father, who commissioned him to be the Suffering Servant Messiah, and who entrusted him with all authority in heaven and on earth, specifically including the authority to administer ultimate justice and to give eternal life.[13] Jesus, therefore, is simultaneously an anti-authority figure and an authority figure; he is the authoritative anti-authority figure.

What does this mean for his followers? We ought to start by understanding the fundamental difference between the rebel Jesus and our rebellious tendencies. We tend to rebel because we don't want to submit; we don't want to be told what to do; we want autonomy; we want to "go where [we] wanna go, do what [we] wanna do, with whoever [we] want to do it with."[14] We tend to rebel because we lack humility.

The rebel Jesus rejected and relativized the authorities of the bogus world system because he humbly submitted to the Father. He rebelled against the rebellious powers because they were

---

[12] Mark 1:15; Colossians 2:15.

[13] Mark 1:11; John 17:2; Matthew 28:18.

[14] This grammatically challenged quote is from a classic 1960s anthem of unbridled autonomy, "Go Where You Wanna Go," written by John Phillips of the Mamas and the Papas. John Phillips lived out his ethos by injecting his daughter Mackenzie Phillips with cocaine when she was a teenager and also by having incestuous relations with her on the eve of her first wedding.

subverting and resisting God's mission to make all things new. He refused to accept the way things are because he was infused with an unshakable commitment to the way things are supposed to be.

Jesus calls his followers to a life of humble submission and humble rebellion. First, we are called to submit, unconditionally and joyfully, to the Liberating King and his kingdom.[15] This is the only logical response to the mercies of God.[16] He has rescued us from the hostile powers of sin and death, and he has made us participants in his new creation. If we believe in the gospel of Jesus, no other response makes sense.

Second, in the context of the church, we are called generally to submit to one another because we fear the Liberating King.[17] This is contrary to our natural inclination to put ourselves first, and is only possible if we obey the command to be continually filled with the Spirit.[18] We also are called specifically to "obey [our church] leaders and submit to their authority."[19] This text must not be used as a pretext to turn the church into an authoritarian community. Church leaders must serve with humility, as stewards who will be required to "give an account" to God, and we must do our part to make their work a joy, and not a burden.[20]

Third, as Jesus' people, we are called to be subordinate to the governing authorities.[21] In context in Romans, this subordination

---

[15] Romans 12:1.
[16] Romans 12:2.
[17] Ephesians 5:21.
[18] Ephesians 5:18–21.
[19] Hebrews 13:17.
[20] Ibid.
[21] Romans 13:1.

is one expression of our unconditional surrender of our lives to God as living sacrifices.[22] This call to subordination does not mean that God endorses all (or even most) of the methods and means of the governing authorities; rather it means that our struggle is not against flesh and blood, and God's kingdom breaks in through revolutionary love, not through revolutionary violence.

A good example of revolutionary love working through subordination to governmental authority is Jesus' command in Matthew 5:41: "If someone forces you to go one mile, go with him two." The "someone" in this passage in Jesus' historical setting probably would have been a Roman soldier or another Roman official.[23] Roman officials had the authority to force a person to carry a burden for exactly one Roman mile (4,845 feet).[24] The Jews in Palestine understandably hated and resented this imposition. Jesus taught his followers to transform the imposition into an opportunity to show the grace of the Kingdom by joyfully going two miles, instead of grudgingly going the mandatory one mile.[25]

Even as we are called to submit to the Liberating King and his kingdom, we are called to exercise the Liberating King's authority as his agents. In Luke 10, Jesus sends out the seventy-two as "lambs among wolves" without "purse or bag or sandals" to proclaim and demonstrate the shalom of the Kingdom.[26] When they returned,

---

[22] Romans 13 must be read in light of Romans 12.

[23] Willard, *The Divine Conspiracy*, 179.

[24] Morris, *The Gospel According to Matthew*, 128.

[25] "The enemy whom I love, the person coercing me with whom I go the second mile, experiences through me the call to accept grace, because my action makes God's forgiveness real" (Yoder, *He Came Preaching Peace*, 52).

[26] Luke 10:1–5.

they reported to Jesus that "even the demons submit to us in your name."[27] Jesus replied, "I saw Satan fall like lightning from heaven" and confirmed that he had given them "authority ... to overcome all the power of the enemy."[28] He then warned them to stay humble, and not to rejoice in their spiritual authority, but in the fact that they have been rescued by grace.

That is where our call to humble rebellion comes in. We are called to imitate Jesus by rebelling against the injustice of the bogus world system and the hostile spiritual powers who operate in and through that system. The bogus world system is characterized by enmity, violence, poverty, famine, disease, greed, and deception, but we refuse to accept the status quo. Instead, we rebel against it by the authority of the Liberating King. We confront the corrupt world system and the hostile powers with faith, hope, and love because we have tasted the shalom of the Kingdom. We must not arrogantly assume that we are competent or qualified to do anything of lasting value from ourselves.[29] We must act on his authority, by his power, using his tactics and weapons, or our rebellion against the culture will be futile.

What does this humble rebellion look like? Three disparate examples come to mind.

This first is a fellow who appears in John's Gospel. We don't know his name, but we do know that he was born blind.[30] The healing itself was simple and organic, reflecting Jesus' authority and mercy. The aftermath of the healing was messy, convo-

---

[27] Luke 10:17.
[28] Luke 10:18–19.
[29] 2 Corinthians 3:5.
[30] John 9.

luted, and semi-hilarious as the religious leaders heard the man's testimony and were bent on un-miracle-ing the miracle. The people who had passed by this blind man daily as he begged in their streets, as well as his own parents, were cowed by the authority and power of the Pharisees. They feared the repercussions of getting on the bad side of the religious establishment. The man born blind, though seeing for only the first time, saw the situation clearly. He spoke fearlessly and even defiantly to these intimidating authority figures. When they asked him again and again to recount the sequence of events resulting in his healing, he replied, "I have told you already and you did not listen. Why do you want to hear it again? Do you want to become his disciples too?"[31] He was thrown out of the synagogue, the social center of Judaism. The beauty of this story lies in what happened next. Jesus, hearing what had happened to the man, turns back to find him. The man born blind submits to Jesus as the Messiah and worships him. This one lowly man truly seeing, humbled himself before Jesus and rebelled against the pseudo-authorities who failed and refused to celebrate the mercy of the King.

The second is Will P. Campbell. Campbell was raised on a cotton farm in Mississippi, studied theology at Yale, returned to Mississippi to serve as a Baptist preacher, and rebelled against the unjust status quo of the 1950s by becoming involved as a circuit-riding strategist and activist in the civil rights movement.[32] This, of course, made Campbell a controversial figure in the eyes of many of his Baptist brothers and sisters, but he was sure that Jesus was against racial segregation and for reconciliation. Then,

---

[31] John 9:27.

[32] See Campbell's autobiography, *Brother to a Dragonfly*.

in 1962, Campbell began telling his fellow civil rights activists that "the racist is the greatest challenge the church faces today in both the North and the South—the most unlovely and the most in need of love."[33] Campbell actually shifted the focus of his ministry to Ku Klux Klansmen. He hated what they stood for and what they did, but he loved them for Jesus' sake, befriending them and proclaiming good news about forgiveness and freedom from "the old way of the world."[34] Campbell's outreach to the enemy made him a controversial figure in the eyes of his fellow civil rights activists, but he was sure that Jesus meant what he said about loving enemies. One of Campbell's former colleagues once asked him: "How in the world do you manage to communicate with those brutes?" Campbell replied: "By emptying the bedpans of their sick."[35]

A third example of humble rebellion is a movement that started a few years ago with a few churches. The impetus for the movement was a Spirit-inspired recognition of a few incontrovertible and obvious facts and propositions: 1) Christmas in our culture has been held hostage by soul-killing hyper-consumerism—serving Mammon rather than God; 2) the followers of Jesus often have been part of the problem, rather than part of the solution; 3) Jesus does not like that; 4) there are millions of people all over the world who do not have access to clean water; 5) Jesus does not like that, either; 6) the followers of Jesus should rebel against the status quo and celebrate Jesus' birthday by spending less money on stuff that nobody needs and giving generously to

---

[33] Frady, *Billy Graham*, 379.

[34] Ibid., 378.

[35] Ibid., 379.

Living Water, a ministry that digs fresh water wells for Jesus' sake. The movement is Advent Conspiracy.[36] The movement has spread to hundreds of churches and has raised millions of dollars that have been used to drill thousands of wells. The rebel Jesus likes that.

Finally, I offer a cautionary tale of Christian activism and civil disobedience. Over the last few decades, one of the most contentious debates in our culture has been about the legality and morality of abortion. Many followers of Jesus (including me) believe that abortion is the ultimate form of child abuse, and therefore must be resisted. In the 1980s, groups such as Operation Rescue organized thousands of people to resist abortions by blockading access to clinics; the inspiration for this strategy was the civil rights movement. However, in sharp contrast to the civil rights movement, through which American hearts and minds and ultimately American laws were changed by the suffering love of Martin Luther King, Jr., and his followers, the abortion clinic protesters did not seem to change any hearts or minds or laws. John Piper, who participated in the clinic protests, explains what went wrong:

> What brought it all crashing down was that it proved to be impossible—at least here in the Twin Cities—to maintain the kind of humble, meek, lowly, lamb-like demeanor of suffering that would win the American conscience like the Civil Rights Movement. The Civil Rights Movement got traction and was sustained because pictures of Bull Conner and fire hoses and

---

[36] See www.adventconspiracy.org.

dogs biting black people and mowing down children with fire hoses took the American conscience. "That we will not do!" But Martin Luther King and the black resistance movement were able to do the miraculous work of not fighting back. King was the key. If others had taken to the streets and done it the other way, we would not be the way we are today. Everybody would have risen up and made war, and it would have been horrible.

But King was able to maintain the control. And the black church had a huge influence. And the blacks themselves had such a long experience of suffering as it was that they had learned how to do passive resistance. And when the hostilities broke out against them, the media caught it and everything turned around.

That did not happen in the pro-life resistance, because pro-life people got mouthy. They were always doing and saying stuff that was ugly. So that's what the media captured. They didn't capture people who were meek and loving and kind being mistreated. They captured pro-life people mistreating. So the whole thing fell apart.[37]

In more recent years, the confrontational and aggressive tactics have been—for the most part—supplanted by quiet prayer vigils and active ministries of compassion to women. This is humble rebellion, loving resistance. Our nation is still divided, but some hearts and minds are being changed—including the hearts and minds of some abortion clinic workers,[38] and lives are being

---

[37] www.desiringgod.org.

[38] See, for example, the testimony of Abby Johnson, a former Planned Parenthood director, at www.abbyjohnson.org.

saved. As Jesus said, some evils can be overcome "by nothing but prayer."[39]

Holy Spirit, give us the humility to submit to your authority and the courage, based on your authority, to rebel against the dehumanizing powers who work in and through the bogus world system.

---

[39] Mark 9:29.

CHAPTER 20

ANXIETY

In 2005, Buddy Miller won the Americana Music Awards song of the year award for his cover of "Worry Too Much," a powerful song written and first recorded by the late Mark Heard. The chorus depicts anxiety as a prison cell:

> Sometimes it feels like bars of steel
> I cannot bend with my hands
> Oh—I worry too much
> Somebody told me that I worry too much[1]

That image rings true for me. When I was a kid, I worried a lot. My brilliantly kooky Aunt Patricia used to warn me that, by worrying too much, I was going to give myself a peptic (I thought

---

[1] Buddy Miller, "Worry Too Much," *Universal United House of Prayer* (High Time, 2004); Mark Heard, "Worry Too Much," *Second Hand* (Fingerprint Records, 1991).

she said Pepsi) ulcer, and that I would have to have some vital organs removed. That was not helpful. For years, I could not escape from worrying about worrying too much and getting an ulcer and losing some unspecified vital organs. To this day I still prefer Coke to Pepsi.

Why do we worry? I think some of us worry because it seems like the responsible and conscientious thing to do. The twisted logic of worrying limits us to one of two alternative approaches to life in a stressful and challenging world: anxiety or apathy. If we don't worry, that means we don't care. If we don't care, that means we are apathetic. If we are apathetic, that means we are irresponsible, and unlikely to be successful. So, based on this distorted perspective, we worry because we think it is the right thing to do; it seems to be a necessary step on the path to success.

Such thinking cannot be reconciled to the teaching of Jesus. In the Kingdom Manifesto (Matthew 5—7), he made it clear that his followers are not called to a life of worry:

> Here is the bottom line: do not worry about your life. Don't worry about what you will eat or what you will drink. Don't worry about how you clothe your body. Living is about more than merely eating, and the body is about more than dressing up. Look at the birds in the sky. They do not store food for winter. They don't plant gardens. They do not sow or reap—and yet, they are always fed because your heavenly Father feeds them. And you are even more precious to Him than a beautiful bird. If He looks after them, of course, He will look after you. Worrying does not do any good; who here can claim to add even an hour to his life by worrying?
>
> Nor should you worry about clothes. Consider the lilies of the field and how they grow. They do not work or weave or

sew, and yet their garments are stunning. Even King Solomon, dressed in his most regal garb, was not as lovely as these lilies. And think about grassy fields—the grasses are here now, but they will be dead by winter. And yet God adorns them so radiantly. How much more will He clothe you, you of little faith, you who have no trust?

So do not consume yourselves with questions: What will we eat? What will we drink? What will we wear? Outsiders make themselves frantic over such questions; they don't realize that your heavenly Father knows exactly what you need. Seek first the kingdom of God and His righteousness, and then all these things will be given to you too. So do not worry about tomorrow. Let tomorrow worry about itself. Living faithfully is a large enough task for today.[2]

Jesus tells us that we should not worry for several reasons. First, it does not do any good. Worrying is the ultimate exercise in futility. Second, it is completely unnecessary. We have a loving heavenly Father. His ability and willingness to meet our needs is evidenced by his care for the birds in the sky and the lilies in the field. Third, it distracts us from the mission of seeking God's kingdom. Jesus makes this same point in the parable of the sower and the seed. The word of life is choked by constant worry.[3] Ultimately, the issue is humility and trust. Do we believe that God is more competent than we are to meet our needs?

In light of Jesus' words about God's faithfulness, Dietrich Bonhoeffer observes that our anxieties are evidence of our senseless and presumptuous rebellion against God's reign:

---

[2] Matthew 6:25–34 (*The Voice*).
[3] Mark 4:19.

The coming day, even the coming hour, are placed beyond our control. It is senseless to pretend that we can make provision because we cannot alter the circumstances of this world. Only God can take care, for it is he who rules the world. Since we cannot take care, since we are so completely powerless, we ought not to do it either. If we do, we are dethroning God and presuming to rule the world ourselves.[4]

Jesus' friend and disciple Peter was there when Jesus talked about the birds and the flowers, but Peter never learned anything the easy way. Years later, after a number of embarrassing gaffes and one monumental failure,[5] Peter has made the transition from being a young, proud, impulsive knucklehead to being a mature and humble leader of the church during the "fiery ordeal" of Roman persecution.[6] Peter wrote the letter we call First Peter to encourage God's people in perilous and challenging times.

In First Peter 5, after giving specific directives to elders and younger people, he exhorts all of his readers to "clothe [themselves] with humility towards one another."[7] This is not a superficial fashion statement. Rather, it is a radical call to imitate Jesus. Peter had a vivid memory of the night that Jesus was betrayed. Jesus "got up from supper, laid aside his robe, took a towel, and tied it around himself ... poured water into a basin and began to wash his disciples' feet."[8] Jesus clothed himself in humility (the towel of the slave) to do the work of a slave. Then he called

---

[4] Bonhoeffer, *The Cost of Discipleship*, 159.

[5] Mark 14:67–72.

[6] 1 Peter 4:12; Michaels, *1 Peter*, 256–75.

[7] 1 Peter 5:5.

[8] John 13:4–5.

Anxiety

his followers to do the same. This "acted parable" points to the story of God humbling himself, becoming a slave, and dying on a Roman cross.[9]

The rationale for this exhortation is that "God resists the proud, but gives grace to the humble."[10] For those who have the wisdom to prefer God's grace to his resistance, Peter continues:

> Humble yourselves, therefore, under the mighty hand of God, so that he may exalt you in due time, throwing all your cares upon him, because he cares about you.[11]

These verses tell us 1) what we should do, 2) why we should do it, and 3) how we should do it, but not necessarily in that order. First, the what: we should "humble ourselves." Second, the why: because God is mighty, he "cares for us," and he exalts the humble. Third—and this is the point that often is missed—the how: "by throwing our cares [on the mighty One] who cares for us." We humble ourselves by quickly and decisively releasing our anxieties to God. In this context, the Greek participle *epiripsantes* denotes the act of making a quick and purposeful throw. At the risk of alienating those readers who have endured too many "drop kick me Jesus through the goal posts of life" sermons, a football metaphor may be helpful here. We should pass our anxieties to God without hesitation, imitating Peyton Manning or Drew Brees—accomplished quarterbacks who get the football to their receivers quickly and rarely get sacked—rather than David

---

[9] Philippians 2:7–8. Jesus, who pre-existed in the very nature of *theos* (God), took the very nature of *doulos* (a slave).

[10] 1 Peter 5:5.

[11] 1 Peter 5:6–7.

Carr—the former Houston Texans' quarterback who routinely held the ball too long and was sacked more than any quarterback in the NFL. If we hold on to our anxieties, we will be sacked by the adversary.[12]

If we fail to do that—if we hold onto our worries and fail or refuse to throw them to God—that does not mean that we are being responsible and heading towards success. It means that we are being proud. It also means that we are being foolish, because only fools would decline help from God's mighty hand, and actually choose to be among those (the proud) whom God resists.

Lord, forgive us for our proud refusal to trust you with everything. Give us the good sense to humble ourselves by tossing all of our anxieties to you. Amen.

---

[12] See 1 Peter 5:8.

CHAPTER 21

MEMORY

I vaguely remember that I used to have a great memory. Actually, more precisely, I was a great memorizer. During my third year of college at Trinity University, I started meeting with an old guy named Joe (he had to be somewhere between thirty-five and sixty years old—all old people look alike when you are twenty) who had been affiliated with the Navigators. Back in those days, the Navigators were famous for two things: 1) they were reputed to be against dating (which is why some folks called them "Never-Daters") and 2) they memorized mass quantities of Scripture.

Joe was not too dogmatic on dating, but he was very dogmatic about waking up early, and he did not want to invest time in slackers and dilettantes. That is why he scheduled our meetings for 6:00 a.m. I showed up at that ridiculous hour because I thought Joe was awesome. Not only had he memorized all of Paul's letters, and Jesus' major teaching discourses (and he was working his way through the Psalms), but he also had been a stock car driver on the dirt track circuit.

Joe inspired me to memorize Scripture, for which I will be forever grateful. I found out that I was pretty good at it; I started with a few flashcards, but soon I was memorizing chapters. Then, for variety and for entertainment purposes, I bought a used copy of *Santa Biblia: Anotada por Scofield*, and I started memorizing passages in very archaic Spanish. I really got into it. I even enhanced my memorization skills by using a memory system developed by Jerry Lucas, one of the very few guys to have played in the NBA *and* memorized the New York City telephone book.[1] Was I obnoxious? Yes, I think I was.

In retrospect, I realize that I was storing a lot of Bible verses in my head, but I was not "hiding the Word in my heart."[2] I was a walking concordance, with hundreds of topical verses neatly filed and cross-referenced in my left temporal lobe. For example, I had memorized multiple verses about humility, sanctification, forgiveness, and prayer, but I was frustrated by a syndrome of pride, entangling sin, guilt, and prayerlessness. Even though I had a great memory and I had memorized hundreds of verses, I misunderstood and missed the real power of hearing and remembering the story of God's grace in the context of authentic, Spirit-directed community.

It took me years to understand the big difference between memorizing verses for the purpose of extracting propositions,

---

[1] Jerry Lucas's first book (co-written with Harry Lorayne) was his most commercially successful, *The Memory Book* (New York: Stein and Day, 1974). He also wrote *Remember the Word* (Los Angeles: Acton House, 1975), specifically about memorizing Scripture.

[2] Psalm 119:11.

and remembering God's story.[3] Luke Timothy Johnson describes the need for the church to be a story-telling and story-hearing community:

> One of the ways the theologian serves the church is by helping it to tell its story. If we only appreciate storytelling as a pleasant diversion, we will not grasp the importance of this function. The study of societies—primitive and complex alike—shows us that although some forms of storytelling do serve a recreational purpose, others perform a more fundamental, re-creational role within the life of communities, shaping both the group and its understanding of reality. This kind of storytelling has to do with personal and group identity. The story of my life—if I can tell it—reveals who I am. Our communal story—if we can give it shape—tells others, and first of all ourselves, how we have come to be who we are.[4]

God wants and expects his people to remember and to remind each other of his story. That is why Jesus instituted the Lord's Supper or the Eucharist. Paul discusses this ancient, subversive practice in First Corinthians:

> For I received from the Lord what I also passed onto you: On the night when he was betrayed, the Lord Jesus took bread, gave thanks, broke it, and said, "This is my body, which is for you.

---

[3] There are many good and compelling reasons to memorize Scripture. I still view it as an indispensable spiritual discipline, and I fully agree with John Piper's essay on the topic. See John Piper, "Why Memorize Scripture?" at www.desiringgod.org.

[4] Johnson, *Decision Making in the Church*, 31.

Do this in remembrance of me." In the same way he also took the cup, after supper, and said, "This cup is the new covenant in my blood. Do this as often as you drink it, in remembrance of me." For as often as you eat this bread and drink this cup, you proclaim the Lord's death until he comes.[5]

Watchman Nee's meditation on the Lord's Supper points out the deep nexus between memory, fidelity, and humility.

> The basic thought of the Lord's supper is to remember the Lord. The Lord Himself says, "This do in remembrance of me" (1 Corinthians 11:24b). He knows how very forgetful we are. Do not think that because we have received such an abundance of grace and experienced such a wonderful redemption that we will never be able to forget. Let me warn you that men such as we, are most forgetful. For this reason, the Lord especially desires us both to remember Him and to remember what He has done for us.
>
> The Lord wants us to remember Him not only because we are so forgetful, but also because he needs our memory. In other words, He does not want us to forget Him. The Lord is so great and so transcendent that He could let us forget Him and not be bothered by it. Yet He says, "This do in remembrance of me," thus revealing how condescending He is in desiring our remembrance.
>
> That the Lord wants us to remember Him fully is an expression of His love. It is the demand of love, not of greatness. So far as His greatness is concerned, He can afford to be forgotten by us.

---

[5] 1 Corinthians 11:23–26.

Memory

But His love insists that we remember Him. If we do not remember Him, we will suffer great loss. If we do not remember Him often and keep the redemption of the Lord always before us, we will easily be conformed to the world and become contentious toward the children of God. Thus we do not only need to remember Him, but are profited by so doing. It is a means by which we may receive the grace of the Lord.

In connection with the Lord's desire for us to remember Him, there is another point worth noticing: as the Lord formerly humbled Himself in order to be our Savior, so today He humbles Himself in asking for our remembrance. As once He condescended to save us, so today He condescends to ask for our hearts. He wishes us to remember Him as long as we live on earth. He wants us to live before Him and remember Him week after week. Thus we derive much spiritual benefit.[6]

There is little doubt that the first-century believers participated in the Lord's Supper when they gathered together as a church.[7] It is likely that the Lord's Supper was integral to a community meal, an *agape* feast.[8] The meal is purposeful and evocative. The story of God's love is vividly portrayed and retold. The breaking of the bread evokes a communal memory of Jesus, who—as the ultimate expression of love—humbled himself and "became obedient to the point of death" on a Roman cross.[9] The wine evokes a communal memory of the blood that Jesus shed for the forgiveness of sin. In this simple meal, Jesus' people take time to remember the entire

---

[6] Nee, *Assembling Together*, 134–35.

[7] Martin, *Worship in the Early Church*, 120–29.

[8] Hays, *First Corinthians*, 193.

[9] Philippians 2:8.

story of rebellion and redemption. The act of remembering, in this context, is not and should never be merely a cognitive exercise. It is a heart check and a gut check, and it draws us into the presence of the Lamb who was slaughtered. The Spirit moves in our hearts as we partake, restores among us the proper balance of humility and gratitude, and motivates us to cruciformity.

If we fail to hear and tell the story of Jesus on a regular basis, then we will forget the story. I am not saying we will forget the facts or the doctrinal points. Rather, I am saying that we will forget the story that must continually shape and re-orient us as we face the unrelenting pressure of conformity to our corrupt world system.

As we remember Jesus' story, we also should remember how his story has transformed and is transforming our story. In the second chapter of Ephesians, Paul exhorts us to remember who and what we were before Jesus made us part of his new creation: "dead in trespasses and sins," we were "foreigners to the covenants of promise, with no hope and without God in the bogus world system."[10] Then Paul exhorts us to remember what God has done for us: "Because of his great love, he made us alive with the Liberating King . . . and seated us with him in the heavens"; "He brought [us] near by the blood of the Liberator."[11] Baptism should serve as a vivid reminder that we are participants in the death and resurrection of Jesus, and we have been set free from the hostile powers of sin and death.[12] Remembering our baptism should help

---

[10] Ephesians 2:1, 12.
[11] Ephesians 2:4–7, 13.
[12] Romans 6:3–14.

us to avoid any proud delusions about our participation in God's kingdom. We were rescued by grace.

Moreover, as we remember the transformation of our story, we may begin to understand how we actually are part of the big story of cosmic redemption. N. T. Wright suggests that:

> [The] main point about narratives in the second-Temple Jewish world, and in that of Paul, is not simply that people liked telling stories as illustrations of, or scriptural proofs for, this or that experience or doctrine, but rather that second-Temple Jews believed themselves to be actors within a real-life narrative . . . the main function of their stories was to remind them of earlier and (they hoped) characteristic moments *within the single, larger story* which stretched from the creation of the world and the call of Abraham right forwards to their own day and (they hoped) into the future . . . They were in a position of a cricketer, about to go out and bat in a match whose long story, and earlier episodes, has left the game nicely poised and ready for fresh action which will bring the story forwards to its conclusion.[13]

Finally, as we remember Jesus' story and our story, we also should remember God's gracious work in the lives of our brothers and sisters. In his letters, Paul often mentions how he is praying for his friends, remembering God's faithfulness to them and their faithfulness to God.[14] This discipline helped Paul to find and keep joy in adverse circumstances, including prison. This discipline will help us avoid the pitfalls of self-absorption.

---

[13] Wright, *Paul*, 11.
[14] See, e.g., 1 Thessalonians 1:2–4.

If we fail to hear and tell all dimensions and aspects of the story on a regular basis, then we will succumb to amnesia. Amnesia, of course, is a "terrible affliction precisely because the loss of the past means the loss of the present as well."[15] If we cannot remember who we have been, then we do not know who we now are. "Forgetting our past means ignorance of our present and the forfeiture of our future."[16] Forgetting our past opens the door to pride.

A friend and mentor of mine, a brilliant lawyer at the top of his profession, was diagnosed with a form of Alzheimer's disease. He was in his early fifties when the diagnosis was made. I remember the day he told me about it. He expressed a fierce determination not to succumb to the disease. In the months that followed, we would get together for lunch. He would tell me about his strategy to fight to keep his memory and his memories. He started documenting every detail of every day with digital photographs. Whenever we met, he would show me all of the pictures he had taken, and he would struggle to tell me about the people and the places in his pictures. He also would tell me about clinical studies and experimental treatments. He knew what was at stake, and he was fighting for his memory. However, the disease was relentless and progressive. Within a couple of years of the diagnosis, his memories were gone, and so was his identity. Do we know what is at stake? Are we willing to struggle to remember?

God, we thank you for the amazing love you demonstrated on the cross. May we never take it for granted, and may we never tire of

---

[15] Johnson, *Decision Making in the Church*, 31.
[16] Ibid.

contemplating the depth of your grace. Thank you for your written word, and may we hide it in our hearts. We thank you for the vivid reminders of the bread and the wine, and baptism. Help us to remember, and to continue to be shaped by your story. Amen.

CHAPTER 22

ENMITY

In the Dallas Police Academy, we learned that domestic disturbance calls are unpredictable and potentially deadly. We studied the dynamics of domestic violence from legal, sociological, and tactical perspectives. We reviewed case studies of calls that had resulted in the use of deadly force by and against police officers. After I graduated to the streets as a certified peace officer, I learned that domestic disturbances calls often arise out of absurd and comical disputes between and among intoxicated and dysfunctional knuckleheads. If you doubt this, watch any episode of *Cops*. Some situations, however, are heartbreaking and terrifying.

I remember one particular call very well. My usual beat comprised the housing projects of West Dallas. Occasionally, though, I crossed the Trinity River to respond to calls in the fashionable and affluent neighborhoods of North Dallas. This was one of those calls. As I pulled up to the house, I was impressed by the immaculate lawn and the tasteful landscaping. The place definitely had curb appeal. The door to the house was open so I walked in without announcing my arrival. I saw a man and woman, and a couple of young kids. The man was holding a knife to the woman's throat. He dropped his knife when I drew my gun.

Later that night, I kept replaying the scene in my head. I thanked God that the situation had ended without bloodshed this time, but wondered how this couple had come to that point. I tried to imagine their story. Years ago, that man probably courted that woman. When the time felt right, he summoned the courage to ask her for her hand in marriage, and she said yes. In front of their families and friends, in response to direct questions from a priest or preacher, they must have made a solemn promise and vowed to love each other for better or worse. They moved into a beautiful home; they had two precious kids . . . and then, one day, he put a knife to her throat.

Scripture teaches that God has created us for loving relationships with himself and with others.[1] Most of us acknowledge that the deepest desire of our hearts is to love and to be loved. It could be argued, therefore, that God's will for us (to love and to be loved) is perfectly aligned with our hearts' desire. If this is true (and it is), why is so much of human history characterized by enmity, hostility, and violence?

There was no enmity in God's very good creation before the Fall. As one consequence of the Fall, God tells the serpent that there will be "enmity between you and the woman, and between your seed and her seed. He will bruise you on the head, you will bruise him on the heel."[2] Throughout the history of the church, this cryptic statement has been interpreted as the first messianic

---

[1] Matthew 22:37–40.
[2] Genesis 3:15.

prophesy, pointing to the decisive battle in the cosmic war between God and Satan—the battle that took place on a Roman cross.³ On the cross, God absorbs and defeats the Devil's enmity. I will return later to this point.

East of Eden, where Adam and Eve relocated after the Fall, quickly became a very rough neighborhood. Adam and Eve had two sons: Cain, the firstborn, was a farmer; Abel, his younger brother, was a shepherd. At the end of the agricultural year, Cain and Abel each brought their offerings to YHWH. Cain brought "the fruit of the ground"; Abel brought the "the firstlings of his flock and their fat portions."⁴ YHWH accepted Abel's offering, but rejected Cain's offering. According to Hebrews, Abel's gift was qualitatively better than Cain's gift because Abel acted "by faith," which—in the context of Hebrews 11—means Abel obeyed God based on his trust in the "absolute reliability" of God.⁵ Cain, by implication, acted "without faith," which made it "impossible" for him to please God.⁶ Cain became "very angry."⁷ YHWH asked Cain why he was angry. Cain did not respond. YHWH tried to get Cain to consider his alternatives: "Is there not forgiveness if you do well? And if you do not do well, sin is crouching at the door."⁸ Cain did what he wanted to do. He "assaulted Abel his brother

---

³ Boyd, *God at War*, 242.

⁴ Genesis 4:3–4.

⁵ Hebrews 11:4. DeSilva, *Perseverance in Gratitude*, 381–83 (discussing the meaning of *pistis* in Hebrews 11).

⁶ Hebrews 11:6.

⁷ Genesis 4:5. In the Hebrew Scriptures, "being 'very angry' is often a prelude to homicidal acts" (Wenham, *Genesis 1–15*, 104).

⁸ Genesis 4:7.

and killed him."[9] Later, YHWH asked Cain, "Where is Abel your brother?" Abel gave a flippant, non-responsive response, "Am I the shepherd's shepherd?"[10] Cain may have supposed that he had gotten away with killing his brother, but YHWH broke the news to him: a witness already was providing testimony about his enmity. YHWH said, "Listen to the voice of your brother's blood, crying out to me from the land."[11] Cain, the murderer, then pled for mercy and protection. YHWH put a mark on Cain for his protection, and pledged, "If anyone kills Cain, vengeance will be taken on that person sevenfold."[12]

Why did Cain kill his brother? The text does not expressly answer this question, but there are a few clues. First, we note that Cain became very angry when God accepted his brother's offering but rejected his own offering. Cain could have responded differently; he could have acknowledged God's authority, and humbly accepted God's decision. He did not do that. Second, before Cain acted on his anger, he could have heeded God's warning and humbly opted for forgiveness rather than vengeance. He did not do that either. It seems fair to conclude, therefore, that Cain's enmity and his violence were rooted in his pride. This thesis—which posits a causal relationship between enmity and pride, humility's enemy—seems to be confirmed by the boastful song of Cain's descendant Lamech, who celebrated his ability to take his own vengeance with violence:

---

[9] Genesis 4:8.
[10] Genesis 4:10.
[11] Ibid.
[12] Genesis 4:15.

> I have killed a man for wounding me;
> And a boy for striking me.
> If Cain is avenged sevenfold,
> Then Lamech seventy-sevenfold.[13]

John Yoder, in an amazing essay on the tragedy of Cain and Abel, observes that YHWH's pledge of sevenfold vengeance "that was supposed to be protection (and in this text is never carried out) has now become with Lamech a matter of pride."[14] The psalmist affirms this correlation between pride and enmity: "Pride is their necklace; the garment of violence covers them."[15] C. S. Lewis echoes these observations about the relationship between pride and enmity: "Pride always means enmity. It is enmity."[16]

James, in his letter to Jewish Christians, offers insight into the etiology of enmity and the antidote for enmity:

> And what is the source of the wars and fights among you? Don't they come from the selfish cravings that war within you? You desire and do not have. You murder and covet and cannot obtain. You fight and war. You do not have because you do not ask. You ask and don't receive because you ask wrongly, so that you may spend it on your desires for pleasure. Adulteresses! Do you not know that friendship with the bogus world system is enmity towards God? So whoever wants to be the bogus world system's friend becomes God's enemy. Or do you think it's without reason the Scripture says that the Spirit he has caused to live in us

---

[13] Genesis 4:23–24.

[14] Yoder, *He Came Preaching Peace*, 60.

[15] Psalm 73:6.

[16] Lewis, *Mere Christianity*, 125 (2001 edition).

yearns jealously? But he gives greater grace. Therefore, he says: God resists the proud, but gives grace to the humble. Therefore, submit to God. But resist the Devil, and he will flee from you. Draw near to God, and he will draw near to you. Cleanse your hands, sinners, and purify your hearts, double-minded people! Be miserable and mourn and weep. Your laughter must change to mourning and your joy to sorrow. Humble yourselves before the Lord, and he will exalt you.[17]

James tells us that the source of enmity and violence is disordered, selfish desire. People lust and do not have; so they commit murder. James then explains that people do not have what they want for one of two reasons: 1) they do not ask, or 2) they ask with selfish motives, in conformity with the fallen world's system. These two reasons have one root cause—a lack of humble submission to the Father who promises to "meet our needs according to his glorious riches"[18] and who calls us to prioritize and promote the interests of others over our own selfish ambitions.[19]

The antidote to enmity, therefore, is humility. James makes this point with a series of imperatives: submit to God; draw near to God; cleanse your hands; purify your hearts; mourn for your sins; then finally and definitively, "Humble yourselves before the Lord, and he will exalt you." This is the way to true wisdom, which overcomes enmity with "justice sown in peace by those who make peace."[20]

---

[17] James 4:1–10.
[18] Philippians 4:19.
[19] Philippians 2:1–5.
[20] James 3:17–18.

This brings us back to Jesus and the cross. One purpose and effect of Jesus' work on the cross was to kill enmity,[21] to "reconcile all things to himself . . . by establishing shalom through the blood of his cross."[22] The author of Hebrews, reflecting on Jesus' endurance of "enmity by sinners"[23] on the cross, asserts that the blood of Jesus speaks better than the blood of Abel."[24] Yoder comments on this assertion: "So we are back to the blood . . . The voice of our brother, of our elder brother Jesus, pleads for us not against us . . . [because] God in Christ loves his enemies—whom we were."[25]

This is the gospel: that God, in and through Jesus, has defeated enmity by loving his enemies,[26] humbling himself "to the point of death, even death on a cross."[27] We, of course, live with the tension of the already and the not yet. Enmity has been defeated on the cross, but enmities persist until the day when God's kingdom is fully consummated and shalom is fully restored. As God's beloved children, and citizens of his kingdom, we are called here and now to be "imitators of God" by overcoming enmity with the power of sacrificial love.[28] This is impossible unless we humbly submit to God, and walk by his Spirit.

> I say then, walk by the Spirit, and you will not carry out the desires of the flesh. For the flesh desires what is against

---

[21] Ephesians 2:16.
[22] Colossians 1:20.
[23] Hebrews 12:3.
[24] Hebrews 12:24.
[25] Yoder, *He Came Preaching Peace*, 67–68.
[26] Romans 5:10; Colossians 1:21–22.
[27] Philippians 2:8.
[28] Ephesians 5:1–2.

the Spirit, and the Spirit desires what is against the flesh; these are opposed to each other, so that you may not do whatever you wish. But if you are led by the Spirit, you are not under the law. Now the works of the flesh are obvious: sexual immorality, moral impurity, promiscuity, idolatry, sorcery, enmities, strife, jealousy, outbursts of anger, selfish ambitions, dissensions, envy, drunkenness, carousing, and anything similar, about which I tell you in advance—as I told you before—that those who practice those things will not inherit the kingdom of God. But the fruit of the Spirit is love, joy, peace, patience, kindness, goodness, faith, gentleness, self-control. Against such things there is no law. Now those who belong to Jesus the Liberating King have crucified the flesh with its passions and desires. If we live by the Spirit, we must also follow the Spirit. We must not become conceited, provoking one another, envying one another.[29]

Father, forgive us for our enmities. Jesus, we thank you that you have broken the power of enmity by your humility on the cross. Spirit, give us the power to turn away from our enmities, to love our enemies, and to live as humble agents of shalom in this rebellious and broken world.

---

[29] Galatians 5:16–26.

CHAPTER 23

ADVERSITY

In 2010, all of my muscles fell off. In relative terms, that was not a big deal for a couple of reasons. First, my muscles were not all that great. They were slightly above average for a fifty-three-year-old lawyer, but that is not saying much. Second, they were not all that useful. In many years of practicing law, I always was looking for an opportunity to resolve a complex legal dispute with a push-up contest or a posedown, but judges, colleagues, and clients generally were reticent to embrace or endorse such unconventional litigation tactics. My muscles did come in handy on that one occasion when a perfect stranger at a gas station offered me a chance to engage in a dubious commercial transaction and then challenged me to a dubious test of strength.

    Perfect Stranger: Dude, do you want to buy some sweet speakers?

Adversity

Me: Dude, thanks for that great offer, but I am not interested.

Perfect Stranger: Don't you want to get a look at them before ya decide?

Me: No, but thank you very much.

Perfect Stranger: Are you sure? They are really sweet.

Me: I am sure.

Perfect Stranger: Do you want to arm wrestle?

Me: Yes, I do.

The muscles were useful in the late 1970s when I was a police officer. After that, the muscles were mostly for show. My muscles were supposed to have been useful in my "50-by-50" campaign (when I was training to get a fifty-inch chest by my fiftieth birthday), but that campaign was a miserable failure, as had been my campaign to bench press twice my body weight by my fortieth birthday.

All of that is in my past. The muscles fell off quickly as the result of an injury. I tore my rotator cuff in the gym. After several weeks of crazy pain and stubborn denial, I consented to surgery. In the process, I quickly lost eighteen pounds of hard-earned steroid-free post-middle-aged muscle. A few months later, my physical therapist handed me a two-pound dumbbell. I could barely lift it. That was sad.

I learned a few things from that season of relatively trivial adversity. For example, I learned that I have a very patient wife whose love for me is not contingent on my muscles. I also learned that I really liked having muscles, and I really didn't like not having muscles. I was embarrassed by my muscle deficit, and therefore I felt compelled to explain my lack of muscles to people who really didn't care about muscles at all (which is just about everybody who has successfully transitioned from adolescence). When I heard myself talking so much about my ex-muscles, I realized that I was not just physically lame; I was spiritually lame—a stupidly proud individual. That is an important lesson, but it is only the opening act for the big lesson. The big lesson continues to be my deep and constant need to rely on God's grace and power.

God uses adversity for redemptive purposes. I am not saying that God is the author or agent of adversity. In this broken and rebellious world, adversity is a given. But God redeems everything, and he graciously uses adversity to discipline us, to build our endurance, to equip us to comfort others, and to teach us how to put our hope in him alone—which is the essence of humility.

Jesus, hours before he was arrested, had a long heart-to-heart talk with his closest friends and followers. At the end of that conversation, Jesus said: "I have told you these things so that in me you may have shalom. In this bogus world system you will have trouble. Be courageous! I have conquered the bogus world system."[1] Trouble is a given, but Jesus offers us shalom and calls us to be brave. Our courage, however, is not based on our own physical and emotional strength or intestinal fortitude. It is based on our utter and complete dependence on the One who defeated the powers of the bogus world system by humbling himself and dying on a Roman cross.

---

[1] John 16:3.

Adversity

The nexus between adversity and humility is a recurring theme in Second Corinthians. Paul's relationship with the believers in Corinth had been strained and damaged because of some self-styled "super-apostles" who criticized Paul for his perceived weakness, his lack of eloquence, his blue-collar job, and his misadventures with the political authorities. They questioned whether Paul had the right stuff to represent God among the sophisticated, gifted, and successful people of Corinth.[2] Paul wrote this letter to explain that his alleged deficiencies were the key to his ministry because God's power is manifested in the humility of human weakness.

Two passages from Second Corinthians vividly illustrate Paul's point. In chapter 1, after thanking "the Father of mercies and the God of all comfort ... who comforts us in all of our afflictions in order to empower us to comfort those who are in any kind of affliction,"[3] Paul makes a cryptic reference to an extremely difficult personal experience:

> For we don't want you to be unaware, brothers and sisters, of our affliction that took place in the province of Asia: we were completely overwhelmed—beyond our strength—so that we even despaired of life. However, we personally had a death sentence within ourselves so that we would not trust in ourselves, but in God who raises the dead.[4]

---

[2] Paul's detractors in Corinth evaluated Paul and his message by the criteria of the broken world system. However, as Paul reminds his friends in Corinth, when he first called them to follow Jesus, they were not wise by those "worldly" standards, or influential, or affluent. See 1 Corinthians 1:26.

[3] 2 Corinthians 1:3–4.

[4] 2 Corinthians 1:8–9.

Paul provides no details. His experience may have been "an imprisonment, a mob attack, an unusually severe flogging, a literal or physical 'battle with wild animals at Ephesus' (cf. 1 Corinthians 15:32), or some other form of persecution."[5] Or it might have been "a flare-up of some illness that was nearly fatal."[6] Ultimately, the details do not matter. What matters is that God graciously used the adversity to teach Paul humility, defined as not trusting in one's self but in "God who raises the dead." This is consistent with the example of Jesus, who endured the extreme adversity of the cross by trusting "the One who judges justly."[7]

In chapter 12, Paul is directly responding to the contentions and criticisms of the super-apostles. He alludes to an amazing visionary-revelatory experience, but declines to boast about it. Instead, he intimates that such an experience may actually produce a deleterious by-product: spiritual pride.[8] Then he describes the antidote to such pride:

> Therefore, so that I would not exalt myself, a stake in the flesh was given to me, a messenger of Satan to torment me so that I would not exalt myself. Concerning this, I pleaded with the Lord three times to take it away from me. But he said to me, "My grace is sufficient for you, for power is perfected weakness." Therefore, I will most gladly boast all the more about my weaknesses so that the Liberating King's power may reside in me. So, because of the Liberating King, I am content in weaknesses, in

---

[5] Gorman, *Apostle of the Crucified Lord*, 294.
[6] Garland, *2 Corinthians*, 75.
[7] 1 Peter 2:23.
[8] 2 Corinthians 12:7.

insults, in catastrophes, in persecutions, and in pressures. For when I am weak, then I am strong.[9]

Once again, Paul provides no details. The stake in the flesh may have been a chronic physical ailment or impairment, or it may have been his "life of tribulation" as an apostle of Jesus.[10] Once again, the details do not matter. What matters is that God even redeems this "messenger" from a malicious adversary. Satan sent the stake to hinder Paul in his ministry, but God graciously used the stake to keep Paul from becoming proud or conceited and to advance the gospel of grace through Paul's weakness.

Given the narratives of Jesus and Paul, it is surprising that we tend to be surprised by adversity. Many of us lead such comfortable lives that we usually see no need to put our trust and hope in "the God of all comfort." Then, when we encounter adversity, we are looking for someone to blame, rather than humbly entrusting our lives to the One who redeems adversity, the One who died for us so that we would no longer live for ourselves.

Lord, we don't want adversity, but we know it is coming. We thank you for using adversity to check our pride, to show us the way of humility, the way of your power through our weakness.

---

[9] 2 Corinthians 12:7–10.
[10] Gorman, *Apostle of the Crucified Lord*, 328–29.

CHAPTER 24

VICTORY

During some of the darkest days of World War II, C. S. Lewis spoke about another war, a cosmic war. According to Lewis, the cosmic war is not "a war between independent powers."[1] Rather, it is a "civil war, a rebellion" against God and his good creation by a "Dark Power," who was "created by God, and was good when he was created, and went wrong."[2] As a result of the cosmic rebellion, the world is "enemy-occupied territory."[3] The gospel is the "story of how the rightful king has landed, you might say landed in disguise, and is calling us to take part in a great campaign of sabotage."[4]

Eugene Peterson describes this cosmic war in vivid terms:

---

[1] Lewis, *Mere Christianity*, 45 (2001 edition).
[2] Ibid.
[3] Ibid., 46.
[4] Ibid.

There is a spiritual war in progress, an all-out moral battle. There is evil and cruelty, unhappiness and illness. There is superstition and ignorance, brutality and pain. God is in continuous and energetic battle against all of it. God is for life and against death. God is for hope and against despair. God is for heaven and against hell. There is no neutral ground in the universe. Every square foot of space is contested.[5]

The life, death, and resurrection of Jesus must be understood in the context of the cosmic war. "When the set time had fully come,"[6] Jesus, the rightful king, the Liberator, invaded the bogus world system, and announced the arrival of the kingdom of God. He demonstrated the liberating power of God's kingdom by healing sick people, un-disabling disabled people, restoring life to dead people, forgiving sinful people, and driving demons out of demonized people. All of these mighty deeds were acts of compassion, but they also were acts of war. At least that was the perspective of Jesus and his first followers.[7]

A delegation of religious scholars from Jerusalem disputed Jesus' claim to be an agent of God's kingdom waging war against the evil one and the dominion of darkness. They proffered a radically different narrative: "He has Beelzebul in him. He drives out demons by the ruler of demons."[8] Jesus responded to this accusation with irrefutable logic: "If a kingdom is divided against

---

[5] Peterson, *Leap Over a Wall*, 122–23.

[6] Galatians 4:5. In Mark 1:15, Jesus announces the arrival of the kingdom of God with the following words: "The *kairos* is fulfilled." In this context, *kairos* means "the appointed time" (Hunter, *Introducing New Testament Theology*, 16).

[7] Luke 11:20; see also Boyd, *God at War*, 192ff.

[8] Mark 3:22.

itself, that kingdom cannot stand. If a house is divided against itself, that house cannot stand. And if Satan rebels against himself and is divided, he cannot stand but is finished."[9] Jesus' argument assumes that Satan is real, that Satan has a coherent kingdom, and that demons are agents of that kingdom. The clear implication is that Jesus—by driving out demons—was waging war against the satanic kingdom.

To reinforce his point, Jesus articulated his mission statement in the form of a cryptic parable: "No one is able to enter a strong man's house and plunder his stuff, unless he first ties up the strong man. Then he will plunder his house."[10] In context, Jesus' message is clear. This bogus world system is Satan's house. In his house, Satan has his stuff—not material possessions, but flesh and blood hostages, precious people created in God's image whose minds have been blindfolded by the strong man, "captives in the Devil's trap."[11] Jesus' mission was to invade, bind, and plunder; specifically, to invade this world, bind the evil one, and plunder his stuff by setting the captives free.

How did Jesus accomplish the mission? The decisive battle in the cosmic war was fought on a Roman cross. The Liberating King, "the Lion of the Tribe of Judah," secured victory by humbling himself to become the "Lamb who was slaughtered."[12] That was the confident perspective of the first followers of Jesus. On the cross, the instrument of imperial terror, Jesus disarmed and disgraced the hostile spiritual powers; he conquered them—not

---

[9] Mark 3:24–26.
[10] Mark 3:27.
[11] 2 Timothy 2:26.
[12] Revelation 5:5–6.

in spite of the humiliating spectacle of the cross—but because of and through the humiliating spectacle of the cross.[13] Jesus—the One by whom, through whom, and for whom all things were created—restored shalom through the blood of his cross.[14]

John Stott describes this shocking victory of the cross:

> Any contemporary observer, who saw Christ die, would have listened with astonished incredulity to the claim that the Crucified was a Conqueror. Had he not been rejected by his own nation, betrayed, denied and deserted by his own disciples, and executed by authority from the Roman procurator? Look at him there, spread-eagled and skewered on his cross, robbed of all freedom of movement, strung up with nails or ropes or both, pinned there and powerless. It appears to be total defeat. If there is victory, it is the victory of pride, prejudice, jealousy, hatred, cowardice and brutality. Yet the Christian claim is that the reality is the opposite of the appearance. What looks like (and indeed was) the defeat of goodness by evil is also, and more certainly, the defeat of evil by goodness. Overcome there, he was himself overcoming. Crushed by the ruthless power of Rome, he was himself crushing the serpent's head (Gn. 3:15). The victim was the victor, and the cross is still the throne from which he rules the world.[15]

The New Testament authors realized, of course, that even though the decisive battle has been fought, the cosmic war is not

---

[13] Colossians 2:15.
[14] Colossians 1:13–20.
[15] Stott, *The Cross of Christ*, 227–28.

over. The kingdom of God already has been inaugurated, but the Kingdom has not yet been fully consummated.[16] The bogus world system persists, and the followers of Jesus live in the dynamic tension between "the already" and "the not yet," between the D-Day of the cross and the V-E Day of the new heaven and the new earth.[17] Many battles are yet to be fought. That is the mission of the church.

Jesus spelled this out during an intimate conversation with his disciples at Caesarea Philippi. Jesus started the conversation with a question: "Who do people say that I am?"[18] The disciples tossed around a few of the popular theories and rumors about Jesus. Then Jesus asked a more focused question: "Who do you say that I am?"[19] Peter spoke right up: "You are the Liberating King, the Son of the living God."[20] Jesus commended the answer, and spoke directly to Peter: "I tell you that you are Peter [*petros* = rock] and on this rock I will build my church, and the gates of Hades will not prevail against it."[21]

Greg Boyd makes three key points about Jesus' statement. First, "Hades was the standard term for ... the realm of darkness and death in Hellenistic culture. As is generally recognized, in using it here, Jesus was probably referring to the whole

---

[16] Ibid., 240.

[17] Ibid. For a brief, helpful introduction to the eschatological framework of the New Testament, see Gordon Fee and Douglas Stuart, *How to Read the Bible for All Its Worth* (Grand Rapids: Zondervan, 1993), 131–34.

[18] Mark 8:27.

[19] Mark 8:29.

[20] Matthew 16:16.

[21] Matthew 16:18.

of the satanic kingdom."[22] Second, the phrase "gates of Hades" is a "metaphorical reference to the fortified walls of the satanic fortress. They are closed to keep opposing forces out."[23] Third, given that gates are defensive structures, Jesus is "portraying the church as being on the offensive and Satan's kingdom as being on the defensive."[24]

Jesus, the architect and builder of the church, tells us what his church is built on—Peter's confession of the truth that Jesus is the Liberating King—and what his church is built for—bashing down the gates of Satan's fortress and setting people free from Satan's tyranny. Boyd's summary is compelling:

> This teaching provides a blueprint of what the body of Christ is to be about. It is to be about what Jesus was about: aggressively breaking down satanic fortresses wherever we find them. In people's lives, in families, in churches and in society at large, the church is to expand the rule of God and the authority of Christ by binding evil and setting people free. In a word, our charter is to live out a theology of revolt, throwing all we are and have into guerilla warfare against the occupying army, the tyrannizing powers of darkness.[25]

How is the church supposed to accomplish this mission? Jesus answers that question a few verses later. Right after Jesus talks about bashing down the gates of Hades, he tells his disciples that

---

[22] Boyd, *God at War*, 216.
[23] Ibid.
[24] Ibid., 217.
[25] Ibid.

he must go to Jerusalem, "suffer many things" and "be killed."[26] Peter, still relishing his role in the triumphal gate-bashing mission of the church, objects: "Oh no, Lord! This will never happen to you!"[27] Jesus rebukes his friend with shocking force: "Get behind me, Satan! You are a trap to me, because you do not have God's perspective, but the perspective of men."[28] The suffering love of the cross was God's way to defeat evil, and Jesus recognized that his friend was tempting him to "avoid the path of suffering."[29] That is not the first or the last time that Jesus would face that particular temptation.[30] After rebuking Peter, Jesus turned to his stunned disciples and told them how the people of the church were going to bash down the gates of the satanic kingdom: by denying themselves, taking up their crosses, and following him.[31] In other words, the church is supposed to accomplish its mission the same way Jesus accomplished his mission: by and through the selfless humility of suffering love, the way of the cross.

There is much that needs to be said and heard about the church's mission in the cosmic war. The following points only

---

[26] Matthew 16:21.

[27] Matthew 16:22.

[28] Matthew 16:23.

[29] Morris, *The Gospel According to Matthew*, 430.

[30] Morris observes that "Peter was taking up essentially the position of Satan in the temptation narrative. The evil one had tried to get Jesus to take the easy, spectacular way and to avoid the path of suffering, and that in essence was what Peter was advising" (ibid.). Jesus subsequently faced and resisted the temptation "to avoid the cross," to meet "power with power," when he struggled in prayer at Gethsemane (Matthew 26:36–40) and when the spectators taunted him to come down from the cross (Matthew 27:42) (Stott, *The Cross of Christ*, 235).

[31] Matthew 16:24.

scratch the surface, but I pray that they will be help Jesus' church maintain God's perspective in the midst of the struggle.

1. The cosmic war is real. The language of warfare may be metaphorical, but the biblical narrative from Genesis through Revelation regarding the struggle between God and Satan is not an artifice or a fictive literary device. It certainly is true that God is sovereign, but God has chosen to exercise that sovereignty in a way that allows free agents (angelic and human) to reject God and embrace evil, to go the way of pride rather than humility, to vandalize shalom and declare war. Paul knew the conflict was real. He knew the frustration of being thwarted by Satan as he attempted to visit his brothers and sisters in Thessalonica;[32] and he knew that the tempter could tempt his converts and subvert or even nullify his labor.[33] Peter knew the conflict was real. From his own personal experience, he knew that the Devil "prowls around like a roaring lion, looking for anyone he can devour."[34] The church at Smyrna knew the conflict was real. John, at the direction of Jesus, wrote to warn them that the Devil (working in and through the Roman Empire) was going to throw them in prison, and that some of them would be executed for their allegiance to the Liberating King.[35]

2. Our struggle is not against people. Our struggle is always *for* people and *against* the hostile spiritual powers.[36] We must

---

[32] 1 Thessalonians 2:18.
[33] 1 Thessalonians 3:5.
[34] 1 Peter 5:8.
[35] Revelation 2:10.
[36] Ephesians 6:12.

differentiate "between the enemy combatants and their hostages"[37] because God wants "all people to be rescued and to come to know the truth."[38] The phrase "all people" includes white supremacists, abortionists, violent Marxists, greedy capitalists, Islamic extremists, militant atheists, entrepreneurial pornographers, that knucklehead who takes up two parking spaces, and each and every person who purports or aspires to be an enemy. As imitators of Jesus, we fight the hostile spiritual powers by loving our flesh and blood enemies.

3. We reject the weapons of the bogus world system. In Second Corinthians, Paul—responding to critics who disparaged his humility as weakness—wrote: "For though we walk in the flesh (= subject to physical infirmities), we do not wage war according to the flesh (= with the weapons of the bogus world system), since the weapons of our warfare are not fleshly but powerful through God for the demolition of fortresses, demolishing sophistries and every high-minded objection against knowing God, and taking every thought captive to the obedience of the Liberating King."[39] Paul's language tracks the stages of the campaign in ancient siege warfare,[40] but his weapons are quite unconventional. His weapons are his humility and his so-called weakness, which means that he relies not "on flimsy human resources,"[41] but on the power of God to demolish the proud arguments of his detractors. This is what

---

[37] Moore, "The Gospel at Ground Zero," 27.

[38] 1 Timothy 2:4.

[39] 2 Corinthians 10:3–5. See also Garland, *2 Corinthians*, 434 (discussing the different connotations of the word "flesh" in this passage).

[40] Ibid., 434–35.

[41] Ibid., 434.

Paul meant when he wrote: "I labor for this [gospel], fighting according to [God's] energy which energizes me with dynamic power."[42] His goal is to capture the thoughts of those who have been blindfolded and ensnared by Satan, "to take them prisoner, which, paradoxically, is the only way to be set free from Satan. Their thoughts need to come under the Lordship of Christ and to be liberated from the captivity of Satan."[43]

4. God's victory is certain, but there is no place in his kingdom for complacency, cowardice, or presumptuousness. The Greek word for victory is *nike*, which also is the name of the goddess of victory. In Revelation, Jesus supplants the bogus goddess of victory, and is called *ho Nikon*, the Victor or the Overcomer, because he defeats the hostile spiritual powers and makes everything new.[44] One recurring theme of Revelation is Jesus' call for us to enter into his victory, to become victors or overcomers.[45] How do we enter into his victory? First, we must humbly get low, submitting to God and boldly resisting the Devil by invoking the blood of the cross and the authority of Jesus.[46] Second, we must proclaim the gospel of the crucified Messiah, which is "the dynamic power of God for salvation,"[47] as faithful witnesses who overcome Satan "by the blood of the cross and the

---

[42] Colossians 1:29.

[43] Garland, *2 Corinthians*, 437.

[44] Stott, *The Cross of Christ*, 246–47.

[45] Osborne, *Revelation*, 122–23. Osborne states: "Our victory is participation in [God's] victory" in "the eschatological war."

[46] James 4:6–11; 1 Peter 5:6–9.

[47] Romans 1:16; 1 Corinthians 2:2.

word of [our] testimony."⁴⁸ Third, we must pray with consistency and intensity. Prayer is integral to spiritual warfare.⁴⁹ Jesus taught the disciples to pray specifically for God's kingdom to come and for deliverance from the evil one.⁵⁰ Paul commanded the Colossians to be devoted to prayer and alert in prayer and commended Epaphras, who was always "fighting for [God's people] in his prayers."⁵¹ Finally, we must persevere. To be overcomers, we must be "faithful until death" and "keep [Jesus'] works to the end."⁵² We must have the same mindset as the victors in Revelation 12, who "did not love their lives in the face of death."⁵³ We must be prepared to endure affliction, anguish, persecution, famine, nakedness, and sword with the confidence that we are "more than victorious" because of Jesus' love, and that the hostile spiritual powers are powerless to separate us from that love.⁵⁴

Pride is not sustainable. Proud cities become abandoned ruins. Proud civilizations become historical curiosities. Proud people face the Truth, sooner or later. In Isaiah, we hear a voice in the wilderness, a prophetic cry, telling us about a day when mountains will be brought low and valleys will be raised up. This metaphor of restoration through reversal is followed by an unequivocal declaration about the harsh realities of the human predicament:

---

⁴⁸ Revelation 12:11.
⁴⁹ Ephesians 6:18–20.
⁵⁰ Matthew 6:10, 13.
⁵¹ Colossians 4:2, 12.
⁵² Revelation 2:10, 26.
⁵³ Revelation 12:11.
⁵⁴ Romans 8:35–39.

Victory

"All flesh is like grass, and man-made glory is like the flowers of the field. The grass withers and the flowers fall ..."[55]

Proud people will be humbled. That is a biblical fact, with abundant extra-biblical historical corroboration. The only questions are when and how we will be humbled. Will we get low now, as a voluntary act in response to clear biblical imperatives? Or will we be brought low later, in fulfillment of clear biblical warnings? That is our choice to make, but we must remember that we cannot achieve humility apart from God's grace and power.

The purpose of this book has been to demonstrate the necessity of living with humility as we—by grace—participate in God's mission to redeem a world that has been vandalized by pride. If you are convinced that humility is a necessity, then you may be looking for practical guidance—a humble plan for getting low. Throughout the history of the church, many profoundly deep brothers and sisters have provided practical direction for us on this topic. I am deeply grateful for their guidance, and I have quoted some of them multiple times in this book because their words are much better than my words.

At least two noted teachers of the faith actually wrote specific rules for and steps towards humility. Benedict of Nursia,[56] who died in A.D. 543, included twelve steps towards humility in his

---

[55] Isaiah 40:8.

[56] Even though Benedict lived as a hermit in the mountains, he was well-known for his piety, wisdom, and humility. In A.D. 529, he founded a monastery between Naples and Rome. In that setting, he wrote *The Rule*, a practical manual for living a holy life (Manschreck, *A History of Christianity in the World*, 102–3).

famous Rule. Jeremy Taylor,[57] who died in 1667, included nineteen rules for humility in a practical manual for discipleship called *The Rule and Exercises for Holy Living*. In these classic texts, Benedict and Taylor organize the material differently and have different points of emphasis, but they are in essential agreement. I have appropriated and reorganized their ideas into a humble seven-step plan for cooperating with the transformative power of the Holy Spirit as we seek to get low.

The first step is to have "a constant reverence for God."[58] Our pride cannot coexist with a proper fear of God. The incomparable Holy One witnesses all that we do. He knows all that we think. That should be enough to keep us humble, but we forget. Benedict tells us to "shun our tendency of forgetfulness."[59] Participating in the Eucharist and praying the Psalms are two ways to cultivate constant reverence.

The second step is to reject our own disordered desires, and to do God's will. This step, of course, is much easier said than done (it reminds me of Steve Martin's sage advice on how to be a millionaire and never pay taxes: "First, get a million dollars"). There is no humility without surrender, but there is no surrender without humility. So we are faced each day with what C. S. Lewis calls "the terrible thing, the almost impossible thing, [which is] to hand over [our] whole self—all our wishes and precautions—to

---

[57] Jeremy Taylor, born and educated in Cambridge, England, is best known for *The Rule and Exercises for Holy Living* and *Holy Dying*, which called on Christians to prepare themselves for heaven by living sober, just, and godly lives (294).

[58] Benedict of Nursia, "The Ladder of Humility," 179.

[59] Ibid.

Christ."[60] Every day, throughout each day, we must pray as Jesus fervently prayed, "not my will but yours be done."[61]

The third step is to cultivate cruciform interpersonal relationships. When pride controls us, we seek to control people, or at least to use people for our purposes. Some of us may do this in a blatantly aggressive manner; some of us may do this in a more subtle manipulative manner. To counter our impulse to control and use people, Benedict advises that we must put ourselves in a position to obey rules and serve one another. The Apostle Paul would have agreed with this advice. He taught that submission is one mark of the Spirit's fullness. Benedict's emphasis on obedience is a hard word for people who do not like rules, and do not like to be told what to do. I know that because I am one of those people. We can start with small, simple acts of obedience to mundane everyday rules, such as traffic laws, our employer's policy manual, and the grocery store's rule about the maximum number of items in the express check-out. There is nothing specifically Christian about such rules per se (in fact, some of them may be arbitrary or downright goofy), but there is something unchristian about our proud tendency to think that the rules do not apply to us. (One word of caution is needed here: if we do obey such rules, we need to resist the impulse to take pride in our compliance. Proud rule-keepers are particularly obnoxious.)

The fourth step is to "avoid drinking the waters of vanity."[62] This is how Taylor describes our tendency to solicit and crave the praise or admiration of others. To counter this tendency, Taylor

---

[60] Lewis, *Mere Christianity*, 197.
[61] Luke 22:42.
[62] Taylor, "The Grace of Humility," 271.

advises us to avoid the "vain noises and empty praises" of flatterers, and to "nurture a love to do good things in secret."[63] With each secret selfless act, we move towards humility.

The fifth step is to practice contentment. Taylor and Benedict both emphasize the connection between contentment and humility. Pride tells us that we can not be content if others have more than we do, but we move towards humility when we learn to be content with our own lot, and even to celebrate the success of others. Pride tells us that we always are entitled to more, but we move towards humility when we express gratitude for what we have.

The sixth step is to confess our sins to God and others. Benedict and Taylor stress that we must be honest about our sins. A proud person resists confession, and may be inclined to minimize, rationalize, or justify sins. Humility requires confession, which is predicated on the faithfulness of God to forgive and restore rebellious and broken people. Each time we confess our sins, we move towards humility. On a related note, we need to learn how to offer timely and sincere apologies. Pride may tell us not to apologize, or (perhaps even worse), to offer a perfunctory "non-apology apology,"[64] but we move towards humility when we honestly say we are sorry.

The seventh step is to speak less often and more carefully. Benedict advises us to "withhold our tongue from speaking,

---

[63] Ibid.

[64] The non-apology apology uses "sufficiently artful double talk" to enable one to "get what you want by seeming to express regret while actually accepting no blame" (Bruce McCall, "The Perfect Non-Apology Apology," *The New York Times*, April 22, 2001). For example, "I'm sorry if you got your feelings hurt by what I said."

keeping silence until we are asked."[65] When we do speak, we should speak "with few and sensible words."[66] Taylor counsels us to resist the desire to disparage others. In our day, there are too many unnecessary and unhelpful words, foisted on us in a constant barrage of tweets, status updates, blogs, broadcasts, and podcasts. Pride tells us that we have a right to express ourselves, but we move towards humility when we listen well and "keep a tight rein"[67] on our tongues and our digital devices.

Of course, there is no easy path from pride to humility. Based on my reading of Scripture and of spiritual biographies, I am convinced that—for most of us—the struggle with pride will continue for the rest of our lives, or until Jesus returns to make all things new. But the struggle is necessary, and not at all futile because God is working in and among us. As we cooperate with the Spirit, as we grow in grace, God will do what only God can do—he will give us the power to get lower and lower, he will use us as agents of his kingdom, and ultimately, when the time comes, *he* will lift us up.[68] Now that is a humbling thought.

Father, we thank you that the battle is yours, that you are with us and that you fight for us in the struggle to restore shalom in this broken world. Jesus, we thank you that you are the victor over the evil one and the hostile powers through the blood of the cross. Holy

---

[65] Benedict, "The Ladder of Humility," 180.
[66] Ibid.
[67] James 1:26.
[68] See 1 Peter 5:6.

Spirit, expose and root out any pride that keeps us from surrendering fully to the rule of God. Give us the humility to invade, bind, and plunder by the suffering love of the cross. Amen.

BIBLIOGRAPHY

Barth, Karl. *Church Dogmatics, Vol. 2*, edited by Geoffrey William Bromiley and Thomas Forsyth Torrance. New York: Continuum Publishing Group, 2004.

———. *The Humanity of God*. Atlanta: John Knox Press, 1960.

Becker, Ernest. *The Denial of Death*. New York: Free Press, 1973.

Benedict of Nursia, "The Ladder of Humility." *Devotional Classics*, edited by Richard Foster and James Bryan Smith. New York: Harper Collins, 1993.

Bock, Darrell L. *Jesus According to Scripture*. Grand Rapids: Baker, 2002.

Bonhoeffer, Dietrich. *The Cost of Discipleship*. New York: The MacMillan Company, 1959.

Boyd, Gregory. *God at War*. Downers Grove: IVP, 1997.

———. *The Myth of a Christian Nation*. Zondervan: Grand Rapids, 2005.

Bruce, F. F. *New Testament Development of Old Testament Themes*. Grand Rapids: Eerdmans 1968.

———. *Paul: Apostle of the Heart Set Free*. Grand Rapids: Eerdmans, 1977.

Campbell, Will. *Brother to a Dragonfly*. Continuum Publishing Group, 1977.

Cole, R. Alan. *Mark*. Grand Rapids: Eerdmans, 1989.

DeSilva, David. *Perseverance in Gratitude*. Grand Rapids: Eerdmans, 2000.

Ellul, Jacques. *Money & Power*. Downers Grove: IVP, 1984.

Faust, Drew Gilpin. *The Republic of Suffering*. New York: Vintage Books, 2008.

Fee, Gordon. *The First and Second Letters to the Thessalonians*. Grand Rapids: Eerdmans, 2009.

———. *The First Epistle to the Corinthians*. Grand Rapids: Eerdmans, 1987.

———. *Galatians*. Minneapolis: Deo Publishing, 2007.

———. *God's Empowering Presence*. Peabody: Hendrickson, 1994.

———. *Paul's Letter to the Philippians*. Grand Rapids: Eerdmans, 1995.

———. *Pauline Christology*. Peabody: Hendrickson, 2007.

Frady, Marshall. *Billy Graham: A Parable of American Righteousness*. Boston: Little, Brown & Co., 1979.

Garland, David E. *2 Corinthians*. Nashville: Broadman, 1999.

Gorman, Michael J. *Apostle of the Crucified Lord*. Grand Rapids: Eerdmans, 2004.

———. *Cruciformity: Paul's Narrative Spirituality of the Cross*. Grand Rapids: Eerdmans, 2001.

Hauerwas, Stanley. *After Christendom?* Nashville: Abingdon, 1991.

———. *The Hauerwas Reader*, edited by John Berkman and Michael Cartwright. Durham: Duke University Press: 2001.

———. *Performing the Faith*. Grand Rapids: Brazos Press, 2004.

Hays, Richard B. *First Corinthians*. Louisville: John Knox, 1997.

Hitchens, Peter. *The Rage Against God*. Grand Rapids: Zondervan, 2010.

Holland, Tom. *Rubicon: The Triumph and Tragedy of the Roman Republic*. London: Abacus, 2004.

Hunter, Archibald M. *Introducing New Testament Theology*. Philadelphia: Westminster, 1974.

Bibliography

Johnson, Luke Timothy. *Decision Making in the Church*. Philadelphia: Fortress Press, 1983.

Kelly, Christopher. *The End of Empire: Attila the Hun and the Fall of Rome*. New York: Norton, 2008.

Kelly, Thomas. *A Testament of Devotion*. New York: Harper & Row, 1941.

Kierkegaard, Søren. "Concluding Unscientific Postscript to the Philosophical Fragments," *A Kierkegaard Anthology*, edited by Robert Bretall. Princeton: Princeton University Press, 1973.

Lamott, Anne. *Plan B: Further Thoughts on Faith*. New York: Penguin Group, 2005.

Lane, William L. *Word Biblical Commentary: Hebrews 9–13*. Dallas: Word Books, 1991.

Lewis, C. S. *Mere Christianity*. San Francisco: Harper Collins, 1980.

Lohse, Eduard. *The New Testament Environment*. Nashville: Abingdon, 1979.

Lovelace, Richard F. *Dynamics of Spiritual Life: An Evangelical Theology of Renewal*. Downers Grove: IVP, 1980.

Manschreck, Clyde. *A History of Christianity in the World*. New Jersey: Prentice-Hall, 1974.

Martin, Ralph P. *Worship in the Early Church*. Grand Rapids: Eerdmans, 1974.

McCall, Bruce. "The Perfect Non-Apology Apology." *New York Times*, April 22, 2001, national edition.

McLaren, Brian. *Finding Faith: A Search For What Makes Sense*. Grand Rapids: Zondervan, 2007.

Michaels, J. Ramsey. *Word Biblical Commentary: 1 Peter*. Waco: Word Books, 1988.

Moore, Russell D. "The Gospel at Ground Zero." *Christianity Today*, September 2011.

Morris, Leon. *The Gospel According to Matthew*. Grand Rapids: Eerdmans, 1992.

Nee, Watchman. *Assembling Together*. New York: CFP, 1973.

Niebuhr, Reinhold. "History as 'Finis' and 'Telos,'" *Readings in Christian Thought*, edited by Hugh T. Kerr. Nashville: Abingdon Press, 1990.

O'Brien, Peter. *The Letter to the Ephesians*. Grand Rapids: Eerdmans 1999.

Osborne, Grant R. *Revelation*. Grand Rapids: Baker, 2002.

Peterson, Eugene. *Leap Over a Wall: Earthly Spirituality for Everyday Christians*. San Francisco: Harper Collins, 1997.

Platinga, Cornelius. *Not the Way It's Supposed to Be: A Breviary of Sin*. Grand Rapids: Eerdmans, 1995.

Polkinghorne, John. *Belief in God in an Age of Science*. New Haven: Yale University Press, 1998.

———. *Exploring Reality*. London: Yale University Press, 2005.

Rahner, Karl. *Foundations of Christian Faith*. New York: Seabury Press, 1978.

Ratzinger, Joseph (Benedict XVI). *Jesus of Nazareth: From the Baptism in the Jordan to the Transfiguration*. San Francisco: Ignatius Press, 2007.

———. *Jesus of Nazareth: From the Entrance into Jerusalem to the Resurrection*. San Francisco: Ignatius Press, 2011.

Seay, Chris. *The Gospel According to Jesus*. Nashville: Thomas Nelson, 2010.

Stott, John R. W. *Christ the Controversialist*. Downers Grove: IVP, 1970.

———. *The Cross of Christ*. Downers Grove: IVP, 1986.

———. *God's Book for God's People*. Downers Grove: IVP, 1983.

———. *The Gospel and the End of Time*. Downers Grove: IVP, 1991.

———. "Pride, Humility and God," *Alive to God*, edited by J. I. Packer and L. Wilkinson. Downers Grove: IVP, 1992.

———. *Romans: God's Good News for the World*. Downers Grove: IVP, 1994.

Taylor, Jeremy. "The Ladder of Humility." *Devotional Classics*, edited by Richard Foster and James Bryan Smith. New York: Harper Collins, 1993.

Thurston, Bonnie B. *Religious Vows, the Sermon on the Mount, and Christian Living*. Collegeville: Liturgical Press, 2006.

The Voice. Ecclesia Bible Society. Nashville: Thomas Nelson, 2011.

Vos, Geerhardus. *Biblical Theology: Old and New Testaments*. Grand Rapids: Eerdmans 1977.

Ward, Graham. *The Politics of Discipleship: Becoming Postmaterial Citizens*. Grand Rapids: Baker, 2009.

Wenham, Gordon. *Genesis 1–15*. Waco: Word Books, 1987.

Willard, Dallas. *The Divine Conspiracy*. San Francisco: Harper, 1998.

Wojtyla, Karol (John Paul II). *The Gospel of Life*. New York: Times Books, 1995.

Wright, N. T. *Paul*. Minneapolis: Fortress 2005.

———. *Surprised by Hope*. New York: Harper One, 2008.

Yancey, Phillip. *The Bible Jesus Read*. Grand Rapids: Zondervan, 1999.

———. *Disappointment with God*. Grand Rapids: Zondervan, 1988.

———. *The Jesus I Never Knew*. Grand Rapids: Zondervan, 1995.

Yoder, John. *The Christian Witness to the State*. Newton: Faith and Life Press, 1977.

———. *Discipleship as Political Responsibility*. Scottsdale: Herald Press: 2003.

———. *He Came Preaching Peace*. Scottsdale: Herald Press, 1985.

———. *The Original Revolution*. Scottsdale: Herald Press, 1971.

———. *The Politics of Jesus*. Grand Rapids: Eerdmans, 1994.